Thomas Balsley
The Urban Landscape

Let's do one together.

Thomas

SPACEMAKER PRESS

Berkeley, California

Acknowledgments

The body of work captured in this book would not have been possible without the support of a great number of people including staff, clients, collaborators, mentors, friends, and, of course, the hundreds of civil servants and community volunteers who have been courageous and trusting enough to travel with me on these journeys.

For their unfailing support and dedication during this critical period of my development, I am indebted to my associates Steven Tupu, Dale Schafer, and Barbara Ito as well as important members of my current and past staff: Jeff Dragan, Allyson Mendenhall, Brendan Higgins, Michael Koontz, Marie Drews D'Angelo, Samuel Lawrence, Chia-Fen Chiang, Shigeo Kawasaki, Benny Ngai, Tran Lam, Stamatios Lykos, William Harris, Peter Dunleavy, Jane Couch, Stephanie Lin, Michael Radner, Illya Alexieu, Joe Sikora, John Burkholder, Charles Birnbaum, Dennis Carmichael, Rich Quigley, Alex Berryman, Richard Slayton, Nancy Lago, Kathleen Bakewell, Tom Wells, Catherine Offenberg, John Priber, Marc Bodewyn, Val Zarro, and Bill Wallis.

I am forever thankful for the timely and invaluable guidance provided over the years by my mentors: my brother, Jim, who introduced me to the profession; Jim Glavin, who kept me on track; and Bob Reiman, George Earle, and Charles Currier.

I am grateful for the rich professional associations and friendships experienced during my seven-year partnership with Jim Balsley and Bill Kuhl, as well as with the clients and designers with whom I have collaborated: Robert Trentlyon, Frances Huppert, Rosina Abramson, Bernd Zimmerman, David Rockwell, Jack Beyer, Todd Schliemann, Bill Bialosky, Eduardo Garcia, Dean Rowe, William Louie, Richard Sullivan, Lee Weintraub, Yoshihiko Sone, Toshininori Teramoto, Yoshiaki Ogura, Patrick Too, George Candler, Soon Kwon, Elizabeth Goldstein, Joseph G. Madonna, Edward Kirkland, Douglas Currey, Donald Trump, Charles Reiss, Adam R. Rose, Paul Broches, Philip Johnson, Costas Kondylis, Wendy Evans Joseph, Burton Resnick, Daniel Reingold, Pierre Gagne, Martha Stewart, Bob and Margo Alexander, Douglas and Maureen Cohn, François Pecard, and Rene Von Maerstetten.

I am extremely grateful to publisher James Trulove and to Peter Walker for their remarkable commitment to expose my work to a broader audience; to Gavin Keeney, the catalyst for this undertaking; to Jane Gillette for her patience and insightful writing; to Sarah Vance for her extraordinary efforts to design and produce this book; and to Allyson Mendenhall, Steven Tupu, and Yang Soon Cho for their advice, encouragement, and tireless efforts to collect, organize, and document the photographs and drawings.

Finally, I want to thank my family and loved ones: Michael James, Gerald Smith, Scott Anderson, Andy Moszynski, and Nina Hernandez for their unfailing patience and support during those long periods of total immersion.

Thomas Balsley

Table of Contents

Introduction
Peter Walker

Throughout the 1980s and the 1990s when most landscape architects were busily expanding in the suburbs or analyzing and defending the wilderness, Tom Balsley was carrying on an entirely different battle—one that is proving of more importance. Coming from a small town, he set up practice—almost upon graduation—in the heart of America's most populous and urbanized city. He was not the first to attempt an urban practice; from Frederick Law Olmsted to Robert Zion, others had tried—and then repaired to greener pastures. Only Paul Friedberg had succeeded in the previous generation, during a time of economic boom and high public interest in urban and social renewal.

Balsley came at a time of economic ups and downs and out of this uncertainty chose a place between the urban developers and the people who make up New York City's many neighborhoods. Here he skillfully carried out a unique career designing the relatively small but intensely needed open spaces that bring focus and contrast to the virtually unrelenting hardness and density that is New York.

Balsley created clients where there were none and found budgets where none had existed, often from the developers themselves. His practice is real, highly political, and artful, and he has made himself a spokesman for open space, the designed public realm, and landscape architecture.

The urban park is modern democracy's greatest art form. Tom Balsley practices park design as such, and he practices it at a time when the very idea of the public realm has fallen into disrepute. Open spaces, once prized, are now to be feared, shunned, or privatized. Or they are to be designed as period-piece antique reproductions, as if to say that our time lacks the stamina to regenerate itself through art.

Frank Lloyd Wright insisted that constraints are an architect's best friend. Working within conditions of diminished expressive potential, Balsley has created islands of hope. He's taken the ignominiously named "bonus park" (so called because, by providing one, developers can add extra height and bulk to new buildings) and elevated it to the philosophical level outlined by Toqueville in the early nineteenth century. Democracy, by Toqueville's lights, is a constant struggle between freedom and equality. If there's too much freedom, the strong will devour the weak. Absolute equality requires total government control. In New York City this struggle is typically played out on the ground. Where, beneath a skyline that has historically symbolized unbridled freedom, does equality dare step foot?

In Gantry Plaza State Park, to mention one Balsley project that has particularly impressed me. Part of a large residential development on the East River waterfront of Queens, Gantry Park commands exhilarating views of midtown Manhattan. The park would be a success even if it were just a series of vacant lots. But Balsley has inscribed the place with a dual portrait of nature and culture in modern dress.

It is named for two immense iron structures that transferred freight from ships to trains. An old power plant anchors the park's southern end. You should go on a day when the light is hazy and walk out onto the four piers that project into the river. Seating, lighting, and other features are recognizably temporary in design, which is to say that they are totems of freedom, exercises of the right to respond creatively to changing times.

Equality tends to come in horizontal forms—parks, streets, sidewalks, subways—and that is the case here, particularly when the piers are contrasted with the inequality manifested in the skyline of the citadel directly opposite. Moreover, the piers colonize the river as a place accessible to all, not just for the occasional ferry ride, but all year long.

In other words, the park holds freedom and equality in something like an ideal state of equipoise.

The gantries themselves have the heroic authority of triumphal arches. This is apt, for they are artifacts of the industry that fueled New York's rise to a position of global authority. As "found" architecture, artifacts that now serve a symbolic function rather than the practical use for which they were designed, they are also tributes to the resourcefulness that has enabled cultural workers to fill the void left by the decline of traditional industry.

Any park can invite you out of doors, into a place where plantings, sky, water, light, recreation, and solitude in public space are the main attractions. Gantry Plaza State Park offers all this and something more. It invites us into the present. Arthur Danto has described public art as a portrait of ourselves, in the medium of artistic transformation. Park designers were making such portraits long before the term "public art" came into use. In this sense, Balsley creates "Society Portraits," not of aristocrats but of the crowds who will come to use them, seeking freedom from the city that towers overhead.

5

6

Manhattan and Environs

● Bonus Plazas

● Public Parks

● Parks as Open Space Mitigation

● Semi-Public Parks

Thomas Balsley
The Urban Landscape

When we fly over New York City it looks as if Manhattan can fit in the palm of our hand. The buildings seem to be made of clay, curiously fragile. If we're not careful we might knock off a spire. In between the flimsy towers there's scarcely room for a toothpick. On the ground, of course, it's another matter. There we are at the bottom of a massive canyon. The buildings are made of iron, and they have nothing to fear from us. And yet, above or inside or on the edge, New York City always looks like *the* place to be, and it can be said that when landscape architecture moved to the suburbs after World War II, the profession left behind a tremendous opportunity as well as an undeniable challenge.

In the late 1960s when Thomas Balsley moved to New York City after college, he both faced the challenge and seized the opportunity. Although in recent years he has developed projects in other parts of the world, especially in Asia, New York City is still Balsley's home territory. And as New York City is only a larger version of many other American cities and, at the same time, absolutely unique, so Balsley is at once a representative landscape architect, and one whose work has taken an unusual turn. Balsley's projects are highly visible. Consider the pyramid of trees on the side of Trump Tower or the five-story waterwall within it. Or One Penn Plaza, directly across from Madison Square Garden, that contains a granite pyramid-shaped sculpture that spouts fog. Or the towering gantries on the east side of the East River. It is also true, however, that Queens West, the site of which is marked by these gantries, is the Balsley project that seems likely to raise his name into the public consciousness. For if Balsley is unusual in having work that is experienced by millions of New Yorkers every day, he is in the same boat as most landscape architects: Millions see and experience his projects, but they do not know his name.

Balsley is a handsome, complex man, visited by the kinds of self-doubts and driven by the self-assurance, goals, and principles that have made a certain kind of New Yorker the hero of a hundred novels. That hero has sometimes been a lawyer, a financier, an artist, a politician, and occasionally an architect—but not, to date, a landscape architect. Tom Balsley is certainly not proposing himself as a

fictional hero, and yet his story—coming to New York, learning its ways, building a practice, honing his art, and then designing public space for millions to enjoy—has a relevance for the landscape architecture community that its unique locale might not at first suggest. In the arena of New York City Balsley has faced the same dilemmas of craft and art, public service and self-expression that have shaped the profession over the last thirty years.

New York City is not only the place to be, it's the place that people come to "make it," to test themselves. It provides anonymity and cultural and racial heterogeneity; it is, in Balsley's phrase, "the lair of the rascal," and it is the locus par excellence of American creativity, one that offers rich opportunities to any landscape architect who thirsts for design challenge and is not afraid of adversity. All of these qualities lured Balsley to New York City. Growing up in a small town—Endicott, New York, home of IBM and a number of shoe factories—he had always known he was headed to Manhattan, known his destination long before he knew what his profession would be. When Balsley was growing up his family kept gardens and orchards for their own use. His paternal grandfather was a farmer, and his maternal grandfather, a German immigrant, worked in foundries, was by hobby an artist, and was the source of drawing and painting lessons—a model for artistic pursuits. This background of factories and farms set the example of making things. Eventually three of the five Balsley children became landscape architects.

Balsley points to an incident in high school as revelatory of his character—and his choice of profession. To the observer it also suggests something about the way that he has practiced that profession. His father had been a baseball star at Syracuse University and encouraged his children to play sports. Balsley was successful in high-school team sports—the guarantee of high-school popularity. Then, suddenly, without consulting his father, he switched from baseball to cross-country and track. "Two things were happening," says Balsley. "First, they were not team sports. I wanted to rise or fall by my own actions. And second, they were both totally invisible sports. Nobody cared who won the track meet." We can also point out a third thing: a conflict between a practical desire to please other people and a pronounced individualism. "I'm very rebellious by nature. I'm also enough of a realist to know that if I'm going to build for others, then I must listen," acknowledges Balsley. These rebellious and individualistic forces may have slowed his progress, but they are also his greatest strength.

Balsley has transformed the paradox of his character into strength—by combining practical interaction with other people and individual idealism, pleasing the group and moving beyond, integrating social responsibility and self-expression—and this merger has played a major role in his career, manifesting itself in his design work. At first Balsley saw landscape architecture as an extension of architecture that was created in a social process via the neighborhood meeting and the client's wishes: He has dealt successfully with the needs of community groups *and* with such individuals as Donald Trump. Now, however, his view of the landscape architect's role combines this same sense of client and public responsibility with a more individualistic vision of artistic expression. Balsley has always been one to listen and mediate, but in the last decade he has begun to listen to his inner voice, convinced of his responsibility as a designer to guide people beyond their own conscious goals to spaces and emotions of deeper significance.

Balsley followed his artistic calling—and his older brother Jim—into the study of landscape architecture at SUNY at Syracuse. Balsley remembers the central message of his education as that of contextualism—that landscape architecture was subservient to its site or its architectural context, that the landscape should be an extension of the architecture. Balsley was also introduced to modernism and the notion that "ideas and beauty could be expressed without literal forms." It was also here that he discovered his desire to sculpt. "I had an early infatuation with Noguchi," recalls Balsley. "I had mixed feelings about this artistic freedom to range through the territory of landscape architecture, but I was fascinated with the possibilities presented by the fusion. It was my first exposure to site art." Balsley's drawings and his design abilities served him well and led to top design honors and the Outstanding Senior Award in 1968.

Because of his financial situation, Balsley's schooling was interrupted every year with work at the landscape architecture office of Glavin and Kotz, where Jim Glavin encouraged Balsley's design talents and his pursuit of a degree. This work-interrupted college career had the effect of enhancing Balsley's educational experience, but it also isolated him from his peers. The three years of practical design experience that he acquired in this way—as well as his strained finances—go far toward explaining why he didn't go on to graduate school: Balsley was ready to hit the boards running. But if missing graduate school was a detriment at one level, his immediate immersion in the world solidified his self-confidence as a designer and uniquely framed his vision of landscape architecture in practice. (Working while studying also brought about a memorable ASLA awards program in 1968, when Balsley won both a professional award and a student award.) When discussing his practical side Balsley is also quick to credit his year of experience working for the Hartford, Connecticut, firm of Currier Andersen and Geda. Charles Currier had done well financially while building a large and successful practice, and for the ambitious Balsley this was encouraging proof that financial security and artistic freedom were within reach and not at all mutually exclusive.

When the individualistic Balsley arrived in New York City he did not think of joining an office, although his brother was working for M. Paul Friedberg. Instead, he set up his own office—a matter, he recalls, of laying his T-square on the kitchen table. In the next few years the architects who saw his sketches and renderings liked them and gave him enough projects to keep him going, but in some ways the early years in New York were stifling. Balsley recalls that landscape architects "could not legally hold a prime contract with the City of New York. We were subordinated to architects and engineers and—except for Friedberg—the old-guard Robert Moses ideas of standardized design, details, and materials with little or no public input."

Of the utmost importance to Balsley's career was that he was living the New York experience: "There are lots of different layers to New York, and it was the sub-layers that I was most attracted to." Balsley was exploring the stoops, the streetlife, and the neighborhoods, getting to know the environment in which he would work and the people for whom he would create spaces. "I didn't just study the city from a distance. I actually lived it. Just as Friedberg found the answer to play through the children and not the administrators, I studied the public open space and its dynamic in ways similar to William Whyte's time-lapse photographic work. Each small ledge, each opening was my testing ground." He quickly learned the symptoms of a failing public space: They looked "neglected and barren," and they were frequently places that had been adopted by a self-defined constituency whose activities discouraged a broader range of activities. Balsley came to recognize that studying the occupants was as important as studying the places themselves: "I've always had a personal interest in cultural diversity and the urban dynamic, and I've frequently been disappointed in my peers' apparent disinterest in understanding and reaching the huge and diverse inner-city open-space constituency."

The value of this sociological design experience cannot be overestimated. Today we see the benefit of Balsley's perceptions in the way that the basketball courts at Hunters Point Community Park are designed for New York City's unique off-court social dynamics; in the way that Balsley's plazas in the Upper East Side neighborhoods bring much-valued water and greenery to their residents; in the way that Fordham Plaza's layout provides a stage set for its impromptu markets and music.

After a few years in the city Balsley acquired two partners. Unfortunately 1973 was the year "the Arab oil embargo hit and all the cranes in New York disappeared." This slump was critical to Balsley's career, however, for with no paid commissions, the new firm of Balsley, Balsley and Kuhl turned to pro bono work. Living in Greenwich Village and later near Union Square, Balsley went to lots of community-board and block-association meetings: "I learned New York City's unique public-review process, its strengths and its shortcomings. And I built good relationships. There are people I worked with twenty-five years ago who are now senior members of community boards." He also got to know the New York City

Planning Commission and staff and built trust there as well. In learning how consensus is forged Balsley acquired the skills of listening and mediating and, of translating both into design. It may be that in later years his strong artistic voice has set Balsley apart from the crowd, but one skill that still aligns him with the profession is this deep respect for the group dynamic in search of the most responsive design.

One of Balsley's major charms—one that would make him a good hero of that New York City novel—is that he is open about his mistakes, chief among which was his isolation from the landscape architecture community and his disinterest in its approval. At the same time that the team-sports side of Balsley was getting to know the public team, the individualistic Balsley was discovering a burning but unmatched enthusiasm for the urban landscape that dissolved his office partnership. He was on his own again, and this time in a more profound sense: "I think I was afraid of being trapped in some herd mentality, and I just went underground on a journey of design and experimentation. Although I studied them, I had little interest in worshipping either the European urban-plaza formulae or the American versions, believing they had little relevance to multicultural urban spaces. I never submitted projects to *Landscape Architecture* magazine or for ASLA awards. Now I can see that that was shortsighted!" This rejection of influence was probably indicative of someone who was still trying to formulate his own design theories and find his own voice.

This frame of mind seems important to document because Balsley's myopia protected a broader vision. It can be argued that his self-protectiveness ultimately kept him flexible, with an absence of allegiance to any one style or dogma—and with an absolute confidence in his own ability to use them all, ranging from classical to modern to organic, depending on appropriateness. His postacademic growth came through intuition and discovery, and his self-protectiveness kept his value system clear: "First and foremost I wanted to improve the quality of urban life. That's still what I care most about." And it also kept him true to himself: Balsley still believes that "no peer acceptance, exhibit, or award can possibly replace the pride and satisfaction I feel from a stroll through one of my spaces that is filled with people from all walks of life. I still find myself judging public open-space design by the degree of the people's enjoyment and allegiance—even if it comes at the expense of design awards." Nevertheless, Balsley now has a long list of influences whom he is happy to acknowledge: at the process level, William Whyte, John Ormsbee Simonds, Hideo Sasaki, and Karl Linn; and in design, Paul Friedberg, Dan Kiley, Lawrence Halprin, Isamu Noguchi, Peter Walker, and the Catalan designers of the 1980s.

Eventually Balsley's time to make his mark arrived: "I'm not exactly sure that I can find a defining moment, but at some point the private development sector in New York discovered me." And they rushed to him because he was listening to them. "I wasn't giving them lip service in the pursuit of a personal design-awards agenda." He understood their goals as well as those of the communities, and he had demonstrated his ability to find a common design ground for both, no easy task in such an activist enclave as New York City.

The venues for these private development forays into public open spaces were such neighborhood improvements as East River Esplanade Park, "mitigation" that was dictated by environmental impact reviews, and the "bonus plaza," a zoning provision going back to the 1960s, but flourishing in the 1980s when the City of New York offered additional floor-area incentives to developers for the creation of new public open space. In return for more floor area (usually height), developers would donate and maintain a fully public urban plaza that in turn had to comply with guidelines set by the Department of City Planning. According to Balsley, the original guidelines produced barren plazas, the only benefit of which was "land banking" for future redesigns, but over time the guidelines were refined and strengthened with requirements for amenities and access, giving teeth to Balsley's design principles.

Working in a city with little hope for new convenient open space, Balsley was one of the few landscape architects to foresee the significance of these spaces and their design opportunities. Since the developers made a great profit on their buildings with the increased floor area ratios (FARs), they usually didn't object to cost. And if they tried to do it on the cheap? "If they want to do something that I think would compromise the quality of the public space," says Balsley, "I can always point to the City Planning guidelines. Most developers understand that a successful park or plaza is good for the city and, if well maintained, can add value to their property. So I'm in heaven because I'm serving a client with a generous budget while also serving the public. It's a win/win situation."

In one year alone Balsley did thirteen bonus plazas, eventually completing more than thirty in Manhattan. He criticizes some of them now because they are too contextual: "My definition of context was too narrowly defined, too literal." But if those plazas lack a strong distinctive personality, he is still pleased with their success as public spaces, and the only real criticism that might be made of them is that sometimes they defer so much to the buildings that they appear private. Such plazas as Manhattan Place, 100 U. N. Plaza, and Shearson Lehman Garden are, nevertheless, more than successful open space; they are urban sanctuaries, gardens in the current intellectual sense: They embed a conceptual notion of nature within an actual manifestation of culture. In translation: They use plants, water, and stone in complicated design forms to create calm escapes from the urban rush. And the good news is that Balsley has been recruited to redesign many of the high profile but barren 1960s plazas, including the General Motors Building Plaza, Paramount Plaza, and Sheffield Plaza, which has been renamed Balsley Park in recognition of his design contribution to public open space in New York City. These redesigned plazas reflect Balsley's new approach to spacemaking and hopefully challenge other designers to follow his lead.

Balsley dates his design epiphany to a trip to Barcelona, Spain, in 1987: There he was inspired by the work being done for the 1992 Olympics. Given his New York experience, he was amazed that "anybody could persuade a city so steeped in tradition to take such a design leap into the twenty-first century." Barcelona's enlightened mayor, Pasqual Maragall, and his consulting architect, Oriol Bohiras, "came up with a whole series of streetscape, park, and plaza improvements for

m

o

The Urban Landscape

14

the city, all the things that I had been dreaming of and was trying to do in New York," says Balsley. In the resulting landscapes he saw "expressions of the human spirit that could inspire and uplift, spaces of modernist order and composition infused with the spontaneity unique to Catalan art and design." Rather than discourage progressive design, these public officials demanded it, making sure that all the bureaucratic hurdles were removed.

Balsley was most impressed with the cultural underpinnings of the design: "The Catalan philosophy of life is a mix of *sena,* common sense, getting things done, and *rauxa,* raucous absurdity, artistic creation." For Balsley it was a transforming experience to see the poles of his personality—and his design approach—seemingly reflected in the design philosophy of a whole culture. As he says, "I felt I was born Catalan." The idea of design that came out of Barcelona was not one of self-centered artistic expression. It was, instead, the idea of a public design commitment. Barcelona offered proof that the landscape architect could integrate art *and* social conscience, design *and* political savvy.

Balsley's more daring design approach in the late 1980s was also due in part to the fact that for the first time in his life he felt financially secure. From the time of his arrival in New York City his concern had been, first, to survive financially and, later, to build a nest egg. But then came the stock market crash of 1987, and it was as if "somebody just yanked the carpet out from under me." He came out of the crash financially and emotionally drained, but with a different perspective: He thought, "Since I'm never going to be rich, why not channel all of the negative energy associated with my fear of poverty toward my artistic callings and the strong design theories that I've formulated over the last fifteen years?"

Balsley's design transformation also came just at the time when he received a series of large, important commissions. Several of these were in Japan—the World Trade Center in Osaka and Gate City in Tokyo, a project that incorporates four colorful Balsley sculptures—but most have been in New York City, part of the movement shared with many other American cities to reclaim neglected spaces, especially the decaying waterfront. There Balsley has laid claim to the design of a number of New York City's most significant parks. Thus the decision to be more daring has had significant consequences, and the transformation in design is observable in the stylistic shift from early work like the East River Esplanade Park (starting in 1984 and lasting eleven years, that project took its design cues from Battery Park City) to such current undertakings as Chelsea Waterside Park, Gantry Plaza State Park, and Rockefeller University's South Campus.

At Gantry Plaza the four projecting piers, the industrial remnants of the site, the vocabulary shift from the land (polished, formal, composed) to the water (rougher and yet more ethereal), all speak of a philosophy no longer attached to the contextual. In an important review, *New York Times* architecture critic Herbert Muschamp rhetorically asks why Gantry Plaza is a "special" place: "Because it reveals the unknown. Because Mr. Balsley has let himself enter into what Gaston Bachelard called 'the poetics of space,' an inner world of images, relationships, discovery, and surprises. The nest. The shell. The miniature. Intimate immensity. The dialectics of outside and inside. These are all Bachelard's concepts. One sees them spatialized here, in a profusion of forms."

Balsley's last decade of work has come out of the conviction that contextualism and traditionalism have been blindly dictated: "In spite of New York's reputation as a global center of the arts and creativity, New York City public buildings and landscapes are painfully conservative products of a well-intentioned public-review process that slowly grinds fresh ideas and progressive visions down to a broth of mediocrity. In the search for consensus and in the absence of successful alternative prototypes, government officials often fall back on the path of least resistance—melancholy references to nineteenth-century landscapes like Central Park. Except for those designers from out of town whose careers are not at stake, this is not an environment that rewards designers who dare to be different. On the contrary, they are usually subjected to slings and arrows and sent to Design Siberia." Such an attitude is detrimental to what Balsley strongly feels is the most important goal: the meaning of the space, "its relevance to our current culture and to future generations, its ability to touch the

human spirit and inspire beyond the bounds of our biases and limited imaginations. We have a responsibility and the potential to play a greater role in shaping the urban environment, a role much greater than just fitting in."

Balsley is strongly against "mindless, senseless form making. My work is still guided by a humanist inner voice that speaks to appropriateness; my work must serve and have meaning. I believe that public open space is sacred ground and that we are obliged to honor the public's trust. It is a rare arena for the acting out of democratic ideals, really a melting pot without any social, cultural, or economic barriers and therefore the ultimate design challenge." The long-term success of any open space that is exposed to the realities of urban life is dependent upon the broadest possible constituency. Designers must listen to "the full range of people whose daily lives are touched by these spaces, like dog walkers and roller bladers, not just those few who comment on 'undesirable uses' at public forums."

Mixed with these programmatic and social convictions is Balsley's strong belief that "there are equally justifiable instances in which we must shock, jolt, slap ourselves awake, trigger awareness, make spirits soar." Using iconoclastic or metaphorical interpretations, his work strongly reflects the cultural image of our times—not just the natural world. "I am always exploring new forms that can redefine the urban landscape vernacular. If our work is to be judged with other great works, it must have something to say and it must answer the question, 'What time is this place?'" Balsley has many ideas for ways to achieve this—for example, the use of the technological advances in video communication. "At a time when television and the Internet have contributed to the decline in public gatherings, the outdoor video screen," says Balsley, "can be the cultural icon that attracts life to abandoned urban spaces, like Holly Whyte's juggler who connects total strangers through triangulation." He also reminds us that sometimes the designer's greatest challenge in an urban setting is to exercise restraint, to curb the design ego in order to let the city's energy express itself: "I try to create stage settings for the great urban performance, spaces that invite people to experience many feelings, live many lives, improvise, stray from their agendas."

The Urban Landscape

The image of the stage seems a central one to Balsley's philosophy for several reasons, the first of which is a matter of process. Balsley insists on the importance of the public approval process—an act of the urban performance writ large: "Design concepts don't come from diagrams. The mixing and brewing happen within. In the public approval process this conceptualization must have room for expansion and contraction, a fluid gel, an outer layer that absorbs, pushes, and pulls, but still protects the core idea. This fluidity can be seen by some as a wishy-washy wavering of principles, but in fact it has become a necessity in preserving the design concept within the constraints of the public reviews." He sees this process as a collaboration (between designer, client, and the public) that nurtures a design idea as it moves from the inner vision of the artist to reality. In ideal circumstances the landscape architect acts as director, assuring the performance of the play while saving the core of the design. As an intuitive designer blessed with a healthy respect for process, Balsley has developed a creative approach that depends upon synthesis of program and site, a brewing that precedes concepts and the expression of forms, one well-suited to collaborations either within the studio, with other professionals and artists, and with public committees.

The second way in which the image of the stage is appropriate concerns Balsley's design work—old and new. Despite their aesthetic strengths the various elements don't stand alone. Whether the new sculptures at Gate City Osaki or the whimsical "follies" out on the piers at Gantry Plaza State Park—the wave bench, the fishing table, the bar stools, the chaises—each element lures the spectator into the space. Railings, seats, sculptures, follies not only define the space, they also transform the passive spectator into actor. In Balsley's work we see formalism as an ordered framework within which forms and objects are juxtaposed, sometimes in harmony and balance but more frequently in search of those fusion points that reside between formal and organic, built and natural, pattern and surprise, *sena* and *rauxa*. And while we can see the synthesis of social purpose, client goals, and artistic expression—an integration of art and meaning in the urban landscape—it is the transformation of human behavior that lies at the heart of Balsley's art: "Most landscape architects are blind to the enormous impact our work in urban spaces can have on millions of lives."

Keeping these words in mind we look at New York with a different eye. When we gaze down on Manhattan from the air we see in the midst of all that built fragility the green form of Central Park, *the* overwhelming fact in New York urban space, the great historic artifact of the nineteenth century. Down on the ground, surrounded by structures that seem overwhelming in their solidity and assertiveness, we sometimes see nothing green at all, and when we do, its design all too frequently speaks of the long-continuing although much-diluted influence of Frederick Law Olmsted. Perhaps we must optimistically see both the dearth of green space and the dead hand of the past as evidence that hundreds of urban venues are awaiting the art of contemporary landscape architects, venues that can become what Balsley calls "the social mixing bowls of a vibrant urban society." Will these places of the future materialize? What will they look like? Will their designers stick to the safe path of traditional mediocrity? Or will they create parks and plazas and streetscapes that continue to make this city "the place to be" in the twenty-first century?

We can be optimistic about the future: Thomas Balsley has been leaving his imprint on the map of New York City since 1969 and his career is only beginning. His latest version of the urban stage may be just around the corner from where we are sitting at this very minute, and we can be sure that it will speak to an exciting future and not to a worn-out past. Balsley has found his own unique design path, but because he is representative of the very best of his profession, there is hope that other landscape architects will be taking their own brave steps in the direction of art.

Portfolio
Urban Landscapes

Project:	**Gantry Plaza State Park**
Location:	Center Boulevard—48th Avenue to 50th Avenue, Long Island City, New York
Dates:	Master Plan started in 1993, completed in 1995
	Gantry State Park started in 1995, completed in 1998
Client:	Queens West Development Corporation
	Empire State Development Corporation
	Port Authority of New York & New Jersey
	New York City Economic Development Corporation
Design Team:	Thomas Balsley, Richard Sullivan, Lee Weintraub, Laura Auerbach, William Harris, Samuel Lawrence
Project Team:	Thomas Balsley Associates, landscape architects, with Sowinski Sullivan Architects and Lee Weintraub; Domingo Gonzalez Design, lighting; 212 Harakawa, graphics

left
**Aerial view of park with
Manhattan skyline beyond**

above
**Aerial view of project site
from Manhattan
A "before" view of the gantries**

Gantry Plaza State Park is the first phase of an incremental 19-acre waterfront park at the Queens West mixed-use development on the Long Island City shoreline across from midtown Manhattan and the United Nations. It takes its cues from the site's industrial past as well as from its environmental situation, creating a narrative that poetically heightens both the cultural and the scientific realities. The park is divided into three areas from north to south: the Peninsula, North Gantry Plaza, and South Gantry Interpretive Garden. The Peninsula is a terraced lawn for a wide variety of activities, foremost of which is enjoying the stunning view of the Manhattan skyline. In North Gantry Plaza this view is framed by the gantries, gigantic structures that once transferred railroad cargo onto barges and are now preserved as ruins. Elegant curving steps form a hemispherical plaza that connects with two of four piers projecting out into the East River. South Gantry Interpretive Garden, from which the other two

piers project, takes form around two paths: one of stone, which passes over a bridge across a small inlet; a second of gravel, which rambles through weedy-looking vegetation and stone blocks. Here there is actual access to the water in a landscape that looks as if it had been abandoned only yesterday.

The piers raise waterfront activity to the level of poetry. At the north, the first boasts a serpentine of seats, a perfect place to wait for the ferry to Manhattan. The second holds a circular lunch counter and bar stools for eating. The third features oversized wooden chaises for stargazing. The fourth is a long wave bench that ends in a table for cleaning fish. While people will doubtlessly engage in the designated activities, they can also experience the piers as intensified, symbolic expressions of waterside pastimes: loafing, eating, stargazing, and fishing. These stages for symbolic action—complete with ruins, a subtle but inescapable suggestion of environ-mental and industrial decay, and the Manhattan skyline as a backdrop—

**Queens West Parks
Gantry Plaza State Park**

make Gantry Plaza State Park theatrical in the best sense of the word. Furthermore, the narrative is enhanced by many details that will reward repeated visits: a range of materials and finishes from the rough to the elegant (steel railings and lampposts, various colors of granite, rough wooden decking, rich tropical wood for furniture and railing caps), traces of the old railroad tracks, a fog fountain, small blue lights that mark where the barges docked, and throughout the park a counterpoint of curved forms that recall the river shoreline with the orthogonal reminders of past industrial activity.

above
Master plan

right
Fishing pier with wave bench

Queens West Parks
Gantry Plaza State Park

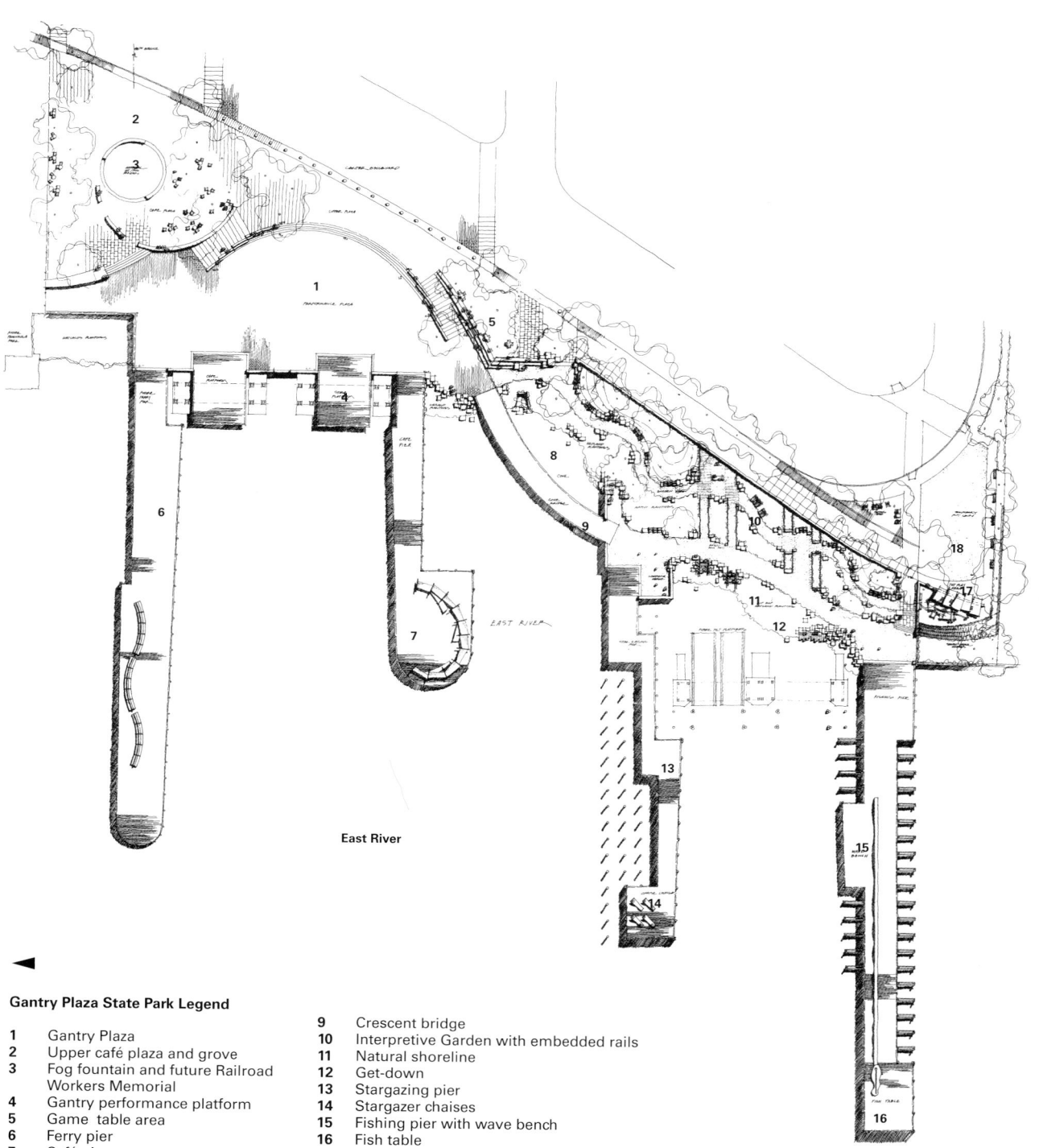

East River

East River

Gantry Plaza State Park Legend

1 Gantry Plaza	9 Crescent bridge
2 Upper café plaza and grove	10 Interpretive Garden with embedded rails
3 Fog fountain and future Railroad Workers Memorial	11 Natural shoreline
4 Gantry performance platform	12 Get-down
5 Game table area	13 Stargazing pier
6 Ferry pier	14 Stargazer chaises
7 Café pier	15 Fishing pier with wave bench
8 Cove	16 Fish table
	17 Play area
	18 Ranger station and public restroom

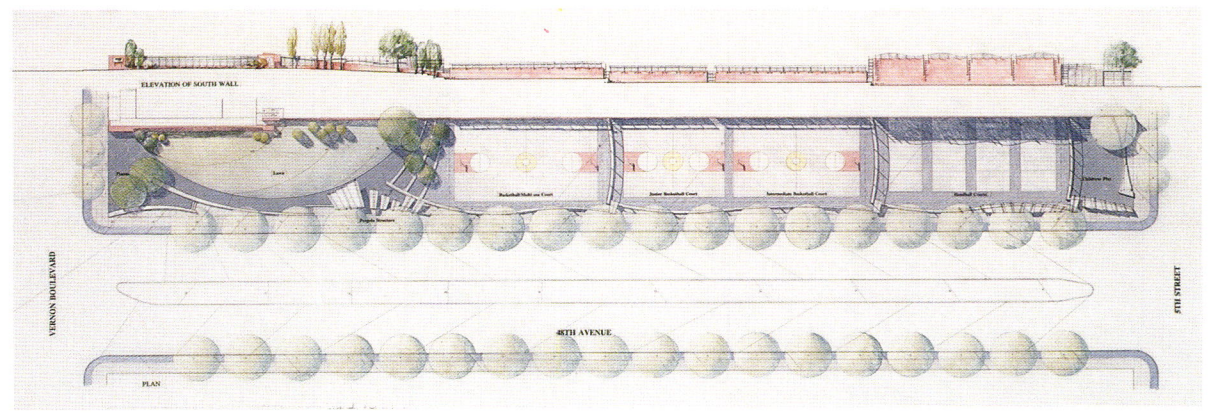

Project:	**Hunters Point Community Park**
Location:	48th Avenue—5th Street and Vernon Boulevard
	Long Island City, New York
Dates:	Started in 1994, completed in 1996
Client:	Queens West Development Corporation
	Empire State Development Corporation
	Port Authority of New York & New Jersey
	New York City Economic Development Corporation
Design Team:	Thomas Balsley, Richard Sullivan, Lee Weintraub,
	Laura Auerbach, William Harris, Samuel Lawrence
Project Team:	Thomas Balsley Associates, landscape architects, with
	Sowinski Sullivan Architects and Lee Weintraub; Domingo
	Gonzalez Design, lighting; 212 Harakawa, graphics

left
**A fluid landscape of walls
and fences encloses the
basketball courts.**

right
**All generations enjoy
the "village green" with
contemporary tables.**

page 30
**Curving terraces provide
spectator viewing of
tournament games.**

page 31
**Street-side benches are
shaded by curving blades
of perforated stainless
steel.**

A 60-by-500-foot sliver that weaves Hunters Point—a light-industrial, blue-collar neighborhood—into the Queens West waterfront development, this one-acre park provides both passive and active recreation in a space that was an abandoned Long Island Railroad right-of-way running through the community to the waterfront. At the east along Vernon Boulevard a crescent of lawn that attracts shoppers and residents segues into the active recreation area that comprises the bulk of the park, ending at the west in a children's play area. The partitioning of these zones is accomplished through a system of colorful low curving walls. The southern edge of the park is defined by a high slate-blue wall penetrated along its length with colored glass block and stainless steel panels. It is a startling device that unifies the park while speaking to the lively culture of the neighborhood, as does the design of the basketball and handball courts. By creating curving and sheltering spaces in front of the courts in place of the traditional chain-link fence, Balsley provides a comfortable place for spectators to group and re-group, a design that accommodates the social patterns of New York City basketball in which the watchers are an integral part of the atmosphere. Throughout this fluid landscape of spaces, edges, and colors in which we experience the changing perspectives of overlapping and meshing forms, the seating, shade structures, and site elements are designed in stainless steel organic shapes with industrial detailing, an introduction to the vocabulary of Queens West.

29

Project: **East River Esplanade Park Phase I**

Location: FDR Drive—36th Street to 38th Street, New York, New York

Dates: Master Plan 1985; Phase I started in 1988, completed in 1992

Client: The Glick Organization

New York City Economic Development Corporation

Design Team: Thomas Balsley, Barbara Ito

Project Team: Thomas Balsley Associates, landscape architects; Manuel Elkin, civil/marine engineering

left
View south from raised podium and pear grove

above
A "before" view north of garbage transfer platform and a "before" view south of parking

In some ways East River Esplanade Park is less a pure design effort than a miracle of master planning. By mid-century the natural indentation in the East River shoreline called Kips Bay had degenerated from such industrial uses as varnish factories and gas works to a parking lot/junk yard/garbage dump stretching from 34th Street to 41st Street. In 1984 a band of community leaders led Balsley among the abandoned cars and rotting piers as they enlisted his talents in an effort to envision a waterfront park and document that vision so that it could be realized. The master plan, sponsored by Community Board #6, was based on the discovery that the area was a series of parcels, each having a different lease condition with a different expiration date. The plan assessed all the water-edge and bulkhead conditions to make sure that a park intervention was possible, then broke the area into parcels according to their lease-expiration dates, delineating costs so that each parcel was "ready to be served up on a platter to whoever might walk in the door."

Within a few years developers saw the housing potential of the East Thirties, an area originally zoned light-industrial, and in order to win their applications for rezoning began looking for mitigation measures (for environmental impacts) or community-improvement packages. Happily, the developer of a building at 37th Street needed a mitigation just as the lease of a parcel of waterfront between 36th and 38th streets expired.

Design problems focused on access, for the site was cut off by FDR Drive, which presented a towering wall to both the residential and park sides. This problem was solved by cutting a wide tunnel/corridor under the drive at 37th Street to create a spatial sequence that provides a delightful explosion of space as we move from the tight street through the covered space to a wide, unimpeded view of the river. The corridor is marked on the park side by two small fountains of polished stone and a plaza created by a cantilevered overlook that extends some twelve feet beyond the bulkhead and gives the impression of a ship's prow.

33

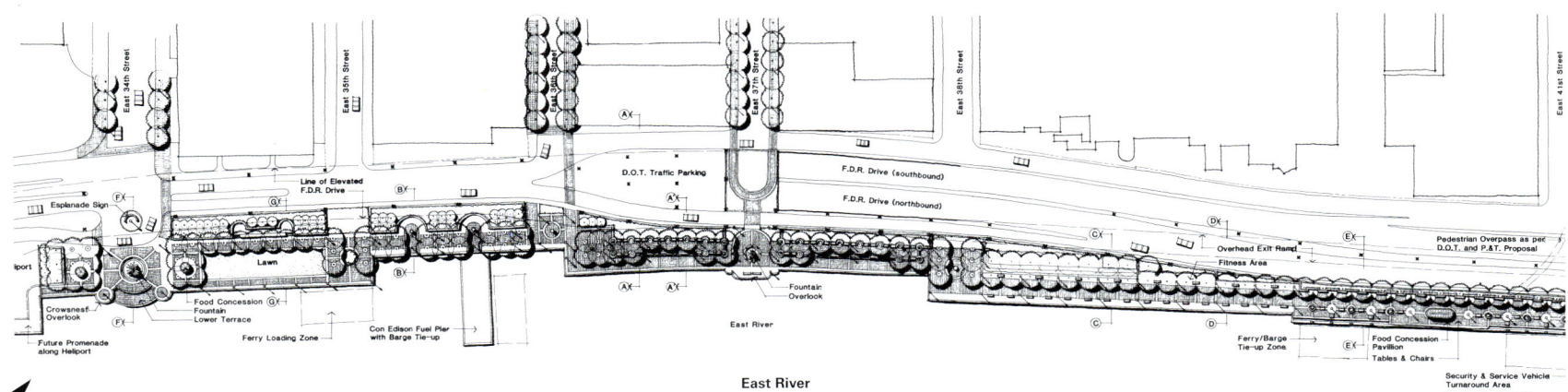

East River

From the plaza at the center the park extends—on two levels—a city block to the south and to the north. One level is the continuous esplanade; the other level is created by a slightly elevated podium under a grove of pear trees. Here the seating offers a view of the river unobstructed by the railing, while the tightly spaced, densely foliaged trees buffer the noise from FDR Drive.

The edge of the podium provides stadium seating and, hence, a variety of social interactions. The community concern for safety is addressed by clear access from the streets and a careful stitching of the ends of the park back into the fabric of the city.

The detailing reveals the popularity of the Battery Park City formula, although it mediates between two popular views: one, that there should be uniform detailing on the waterfront parks to tie together the diverse architectural edge; the other, that the esplanades themselves provide continuity so that each section can take on its own personality. Here, the use of the World's Fair bench, cobblestones, the distinctive leaning railing, and lampposts borrowed from Central Park speak the Battery Park City vocabulary, but Balsley also uses brick, sandblasted precast detailings, and stone in historical ways.

left
View north along esplanade and overlook

above
Detail across fountain weir to overlook and Queens beyond

Project: **Gate City Osaki**

Location: Tokyo, Japan

Dates: Started in 1997, completed in 1999

Client: Mitsui Fudosan Co., Ltd.

Design Team: Thomas Balsley, Steven Tupu, Keith Crawford, Shigeo Kawasaki

Project Team: Thomas Balsley Associates, landscape architects; Nikken Sekkei, architects; LPA Inc., lighting; Thomas Balsley and Steven Tupu, sculpture design

left
Grove **sculpture rests on a geometric carpet of green and white granite.**

right from top
Fastigiate juniper terminate one triangular grove panel.

Orange lattice panels provide a foil for the auto drop-off area.

For this mixed-use development in Osaki on the outskirts of Tokyo, Balsley designed a public plaza that is the main entry to the complex, as well as a public garden linking the complex to the residential neighborhood to the north.

The entry plaza, extremely visible because of its location across from a train station, features two groves of trees planted in grids: one, a grove of living trees; the other, abstract sculpture recalling trees. The plaza is covered with a paving of gray and white granite in a strong geometrical pattern of parallelograms that take their angles from the triangular beds of trees. (The two that hold the living trees can be visually joined into another parallelogram.) On the same angle slicing

through the living grove are cuts of paving or channels of water (also parallelograms), several of the water channels emptying into an asymmetrical pool with an aerated edge that creates a line of foam. The grove is studded with stone monoliths with a parallelogram footprint. The second grove, in a grid but with a less articulated ground, is of orange columns that point in a number of directions. The two groves are placed so that pedestrians heading toward the escalators will pass between them and experience the crossfire between leaning orange columns and upright trees. Dark charcoal granite, sometimes polished, sometimes honed, creates a sharply articulated edge for the geometric forms and the pavement and water channels that penetrate the living grove. This stunning entry plaza has recently served as the opening scene for one of Japan's most popular television shows.

The North Garden links the development to the adjacent neighborhood, which lies across a canal. Pedestrians can enter the garden along a footbridge over the canal or

37

Gate City Osaki

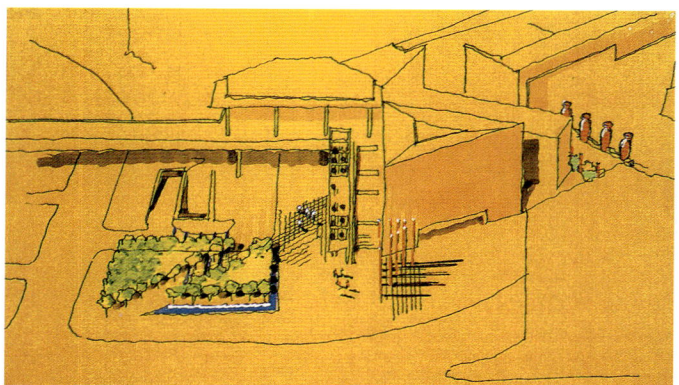

Concept study sketch

page 40
Glass-block runnel leading to *Calla* folly and perforated seating

page 41
An evening view from the North Garden plaza and glowing glass-block fountain to the *Phragmites* folly beyond

page 42
***Calla* folly**

page 43
***Carex* folly blades piercing the sky**

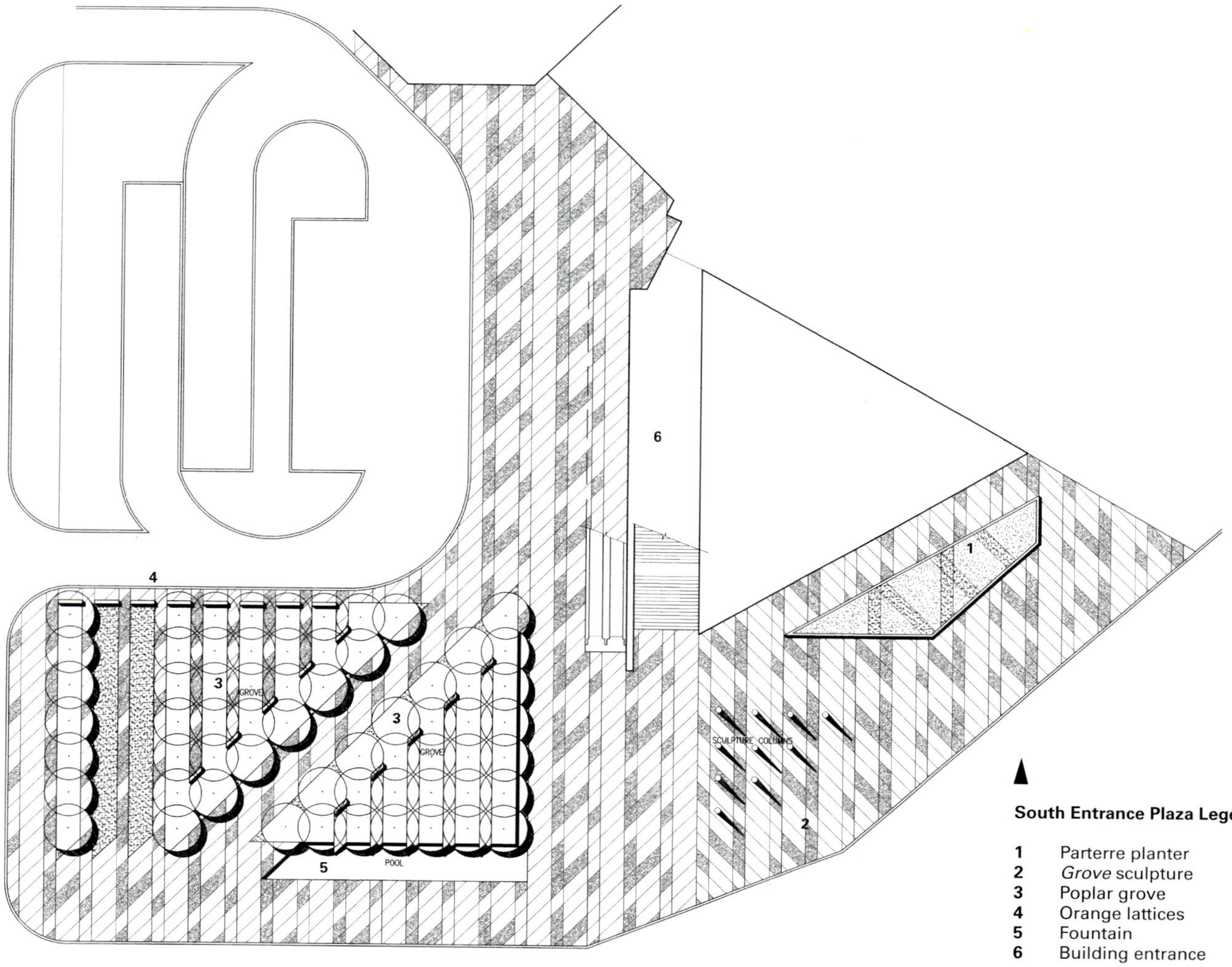

38

GROVE

GROVE

SCULPTURE COLUMNS

POOL

South Entrance Plaza Legend

1	Parterre planter
2	*Grove* sculpture
3	Poplar grove
4	Orange lattices
5	Fountain
6	Building entrance

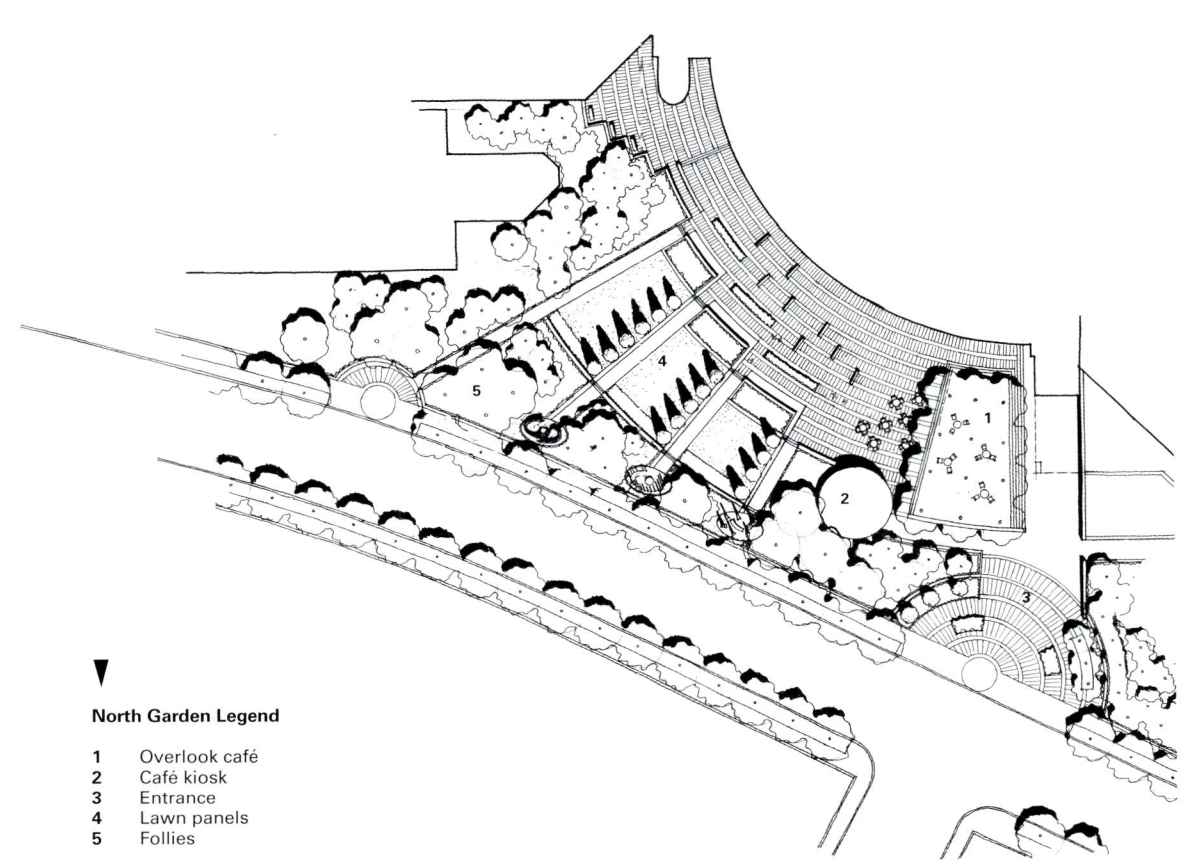

North Garden Legend

1   Overlook café
2   Café kiosk
3   Entrance
4   Lawn panels
5   Follies

Poplar grove and water channels

through the building's atrium, which is called the Winter Garden. The garden takes its cues from the circular form of the atrium and provides a sequence of environments that can accommodate both large gatherings of people and secluded couples. The area near the Winter Garden is paved in a radiating pattern. Paths also radiate from the wall to the outer edges of the garden. Each path is edged in frosted glass block with fiber-optic lighting. Near the building the paving is punctuated with distinctive seats, granite slabs that appear to float over their perforated stainless steel bases. At the edge of the garden to the west is an elevated podium, again richly paved, with tables and chairs in a grove of shade trees. To the east are three follies and, at the far east, a more naturalistic garden that takes its cues from the Japanese.

The follies, the high point of the project, are foreshadowed by the orange column grove of metaphorical trees in the entry plaza. Each folly is conceived on a botanical theme, each derived from a different degree of spatial enclosure. The chartreuse yellow folly, *Carex,* explores space that lacks a complete physical surround. The central folly, *Phragmites,* provides a greater sense of enclosure, while the spacing and slant of its fuschia columns suggest the force of a blowing wind. The third folly is *Calla*, two dark gray petals wrapped in a dance that suggests a solid enclosure. Again, as in the entry plaza, the experience of the space develops from a contrast between the artificial folly in vegetative form—a grass, a reed, and a lily—and the greener, living surround.

Project: **World Trade Center Osaka**

Location: Osaka, Japan

Dates: Started in 1992, completed in 1996

Client: World Trade Center Associates

              Nikken Sekkei

Design Team: Thomas Balsley, Nancy Lago

Project Team: Thomas Balsley Associates, landscape architects; Nikken Sekkei, Mancini Duffy, architects; LPA Inc., lighting; Thomas Balsley, sculpture design

Thomas Balsley Associates joined the design team at a point when many of the decisions about the development of the World Trade Center had already been made, decisions that structured efforts to create a parklike environment at the base of one of Osaka's tallest buildings. The space was divided, so unifying the whole design was a central issue. The most intrusive elements were the rows of concrete ventilation towers rising from the structure below. In the North Garden these were transformed into a performance stage structure, while the six in the South Court were incorporated into a fountain as stainless steel cones rising like the noses of rockets out of a lagoon. Elevating the park by some three feet allowed planting without containers throughout, as well as an intriguing display of falling water in the stand-out feature, the South Court fountain of the cones.

The plaza's fountain edge is expressed as a crescent of stepped edges over which the water cascades in carefully modulated waves into a lower pool, which in turn forms a crescent in a circular terrace detailed in alternating rings of dark and light pavers. The pool edge has been detailed with whimsical red spheres.

Beyond the edge of the pool a more relaxed series of curves creates a series of coves and peninsulas planted with dogwoods and pine trees, a frame that softens and enhances the mysterious cones.

The water falls down the stepped slope from the lagoon as sheets of water rather than as a waterfall. The fountain's edge on the street side is detailed as a slope of polished black granite that contains a geometrical formation of stainless steel pipes, stone, and water, creating a complement to the stainless steel cones above. The perforations in the cones emit mist in summer, fog and steam in winter, and the whole is bathed in a red glow at night, a suitable futuristic addition to the city of Osaka, which calls itself "Cosmos City" in a celebration of space technology.

45

left
Mist, water, Japanese pines and cone sculptures

right from top
Entrance to South Court

Impromptu seating at fountain edge

◄

46 **World Trade Center Osaka**
Legend

1 South Court
2 Cone sculpture
3 Café terrace
4 All-weather park (not built)
5 North Garden
6 Performance area
7 Glass-block ventilation tower
8 Gardens

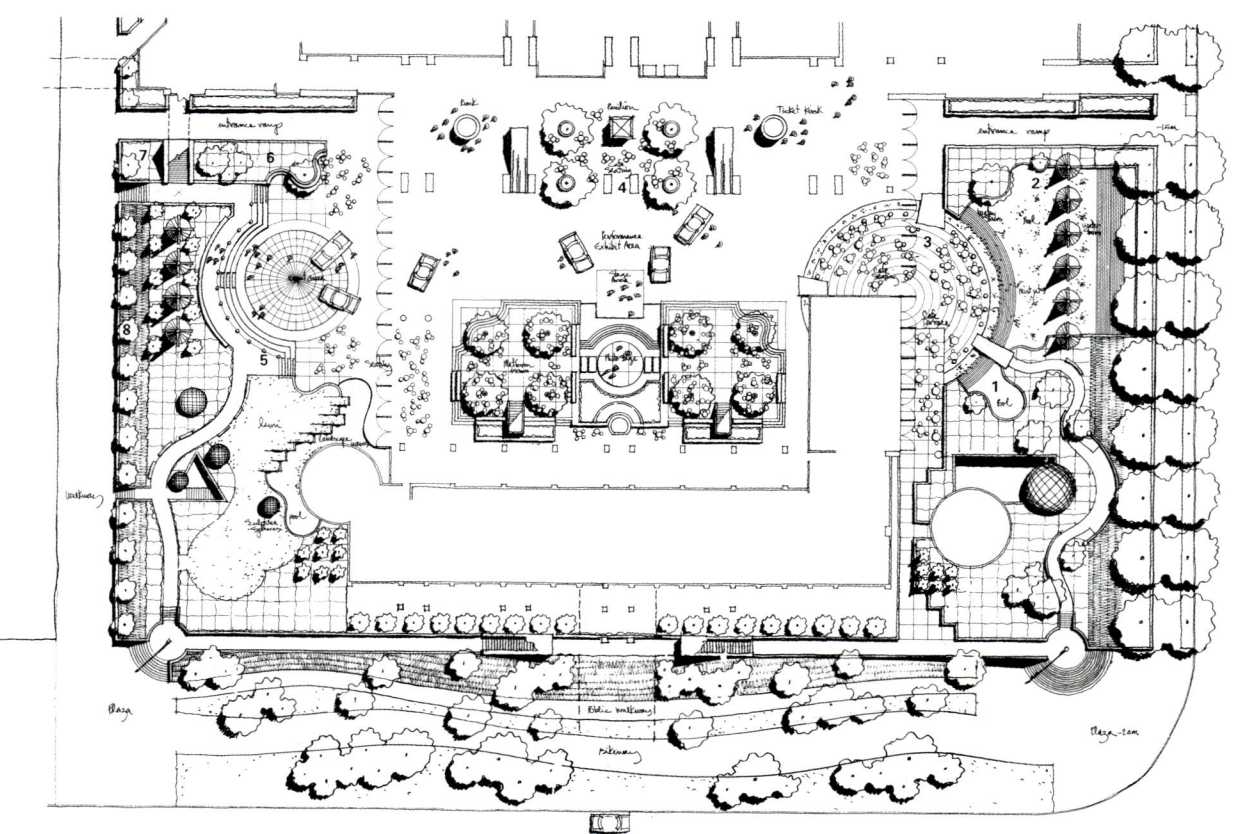

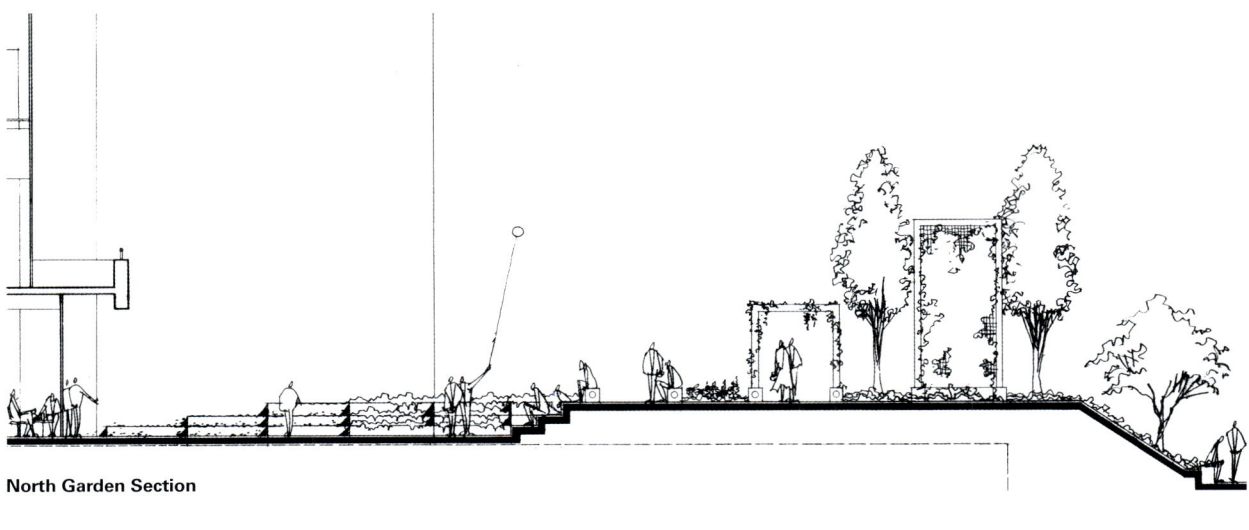

North Garden Section

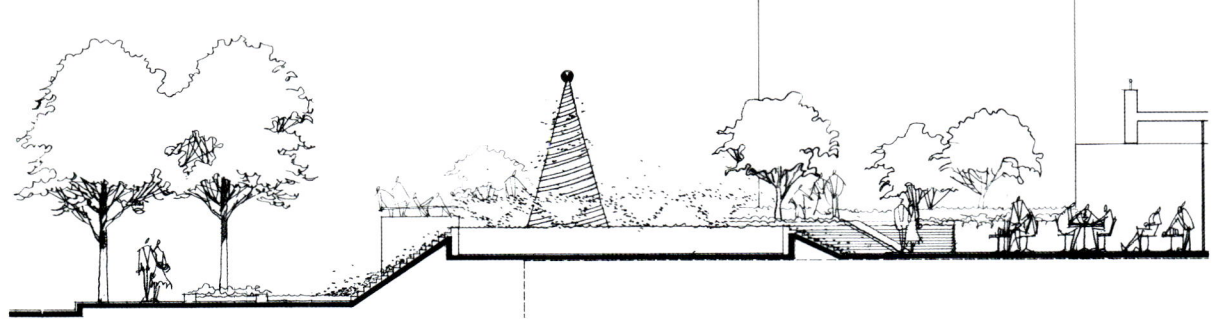

South Court Section

page 46 from left
Waves washing into the café terrace pool

View from street of South Court fountain slope and pipe inserts

North Garden performance circle washed with the glow of glass-block ventilation towers

above from left
South Court fountain stairway

North Garden terraces

South Court café

page 48
Dramatic lighting reveals the random perforations and red interiors of the cones.

Project: **Progressive Insurance Corporate Headquarters**
Location: Cleveland, Ohio
Dates: Started in 1991, completed in 1995
Client: Progressive Insurance Company
Design Team: Thomas Balsley, Stephanie Lin, Michael Radner
Project Team: Thomas Balsley Associates, landscape architects;
                     William Bialosky/Bialosky and Partners, Keeva Kekst, architects;
                     H. M. Brandston & Partners, Inc., lighting

This corporate campus in Cleveland, Ohio, is sited within a natural woodland, punctuated with ravines, dry streambeds, and companion beech and birch stands. The facility's size—one million square feet—is broken down into smaller programmatic components, which, in turn, are expressed in two linear building forms connected by enclosed walkways at two locations and divided by a continuous courtyard. The building's square footage also generates extensive parking needs, which are accommodated in perimeter parking structures in order to preserve open space.

The courtyard garden reinterprets the site's natural features in the form of a "ravine" that exposes the occupants, particularly those in offices with central orientations, to such natural phenomena as seasonal changes. Precast walls and bands extend the building's geometry into the site; intersecting curving pathways are expressed in strong paving patterns in alternating colors. This linear composition of built forms engages the courtyard landscape in a series of modulated moments of tension and harmony, sometimes expressed in the pathway's broken edge along the dry "streambed" or with walls extending from planter berms. Along the way are programmed spaces for café tables, outdoor conference spaces, and entrances. Seasonal plantings and perennial beds add color and scale to the visual experience, especially from above.

This strongly linear landscape culminates in a symbolic birch grove on a grid. The cafeteria terrace enjoys unobstructed views and access to the site's natural ravine, stream, and walking trails. The purposeful transition from metaphor to reality compels the viewers to consider the place of the designed landscape in the natural environment and to engage in the provocative struggle for balance.

51

left
**Precast-concrete terrace walls
collide with the free-form path.**

**Progressive Insurance
Corporate Headquarters**

52   **Progressive Insurance Corporate
Headquarters Legend**

1	Entrance plaza
2	Birch grove
3	North court
4	Stream path
5	Roof terrace
6	Central court
7	Terrace lawn
8	Cafeteria
9	Cafeteria terrace
10	South court

right
**Upper garden terrace and
outdoor conference "pods"
overlook the garden path edged
with broken pavers and set in a
stream of gravel.**

page 54
**Serpentine path with broken
edge along gravel "stream"**

Portfolio
Visionary Landscapes

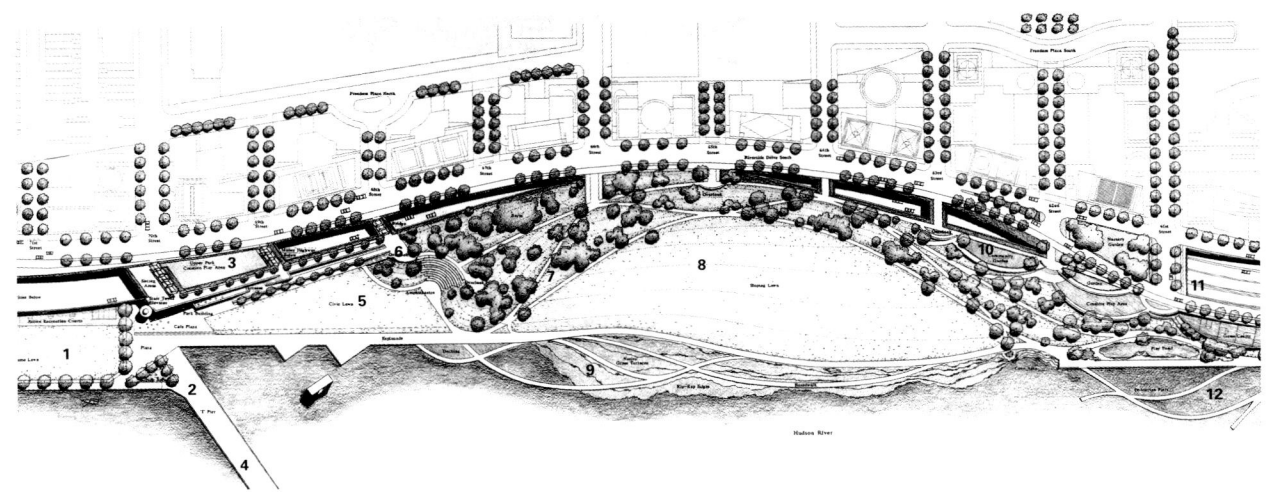

▲

**Riverside South Park
Legend**

1 Sports field
2 Plaza
3 Overlook park
4 Pier I
5 Civic lawn
6 Amphitheater
7 Promontory
8 Great lawn
9 Marsh paths
10 Play area
11 Community gardens
12 Serpentine walkways

Project: **Riverside South Park**

Location: Hudson River—59th Street to 72nd Street
New York, New York

Dates: Started in 1991, completed in 1992

Client: Riverside South Planning Corporation

Project Team: Thomas Balsley Associates, landscape architects;
Skidmore Owings & Merrill and Paul Willen, architects

The Riverside South development stretches along the Hudson River from 59th Street to 72nd Street on what was a major rail transfer point at the turn of the century. Balsley was asked to lead the collaborative design team in developing a plan for the project's centerpiece, a 21-acre waterfront park. This coordinated design effort, involving urban design, environmental considerations, and highway relocation, required a creative, yet highly efficient design approach that was responsive to intractable timetables as well as agency comments, community participation, and client objectives. Numerous meet-

ings and presentations with community groups and public agencies were conducted so that the design properly reflected community needs.

The park design strives to transform this piece of the Hudson River shoreline into a waterfront park unique to Manhattan, expressive of its industrial and transportation heritage, yet ecologically sensitive to its river-edge environment. The plan to relocate the existing Miller Highway beneath the proposed Riverside Drive South extension allows city residents to connect directly to park and river without having to cross the West Side Highway. As extensions of each street corridor, park entrance foyers are enriched with trellises and offer secure seating areas with dramatic views. The 40-foot grade change from the street becomes a dramatic descent to the river along natural walkways, terraced overlooks, stairways, and an elevator at the café entrance at 70th Street. Esplanades,

boardwalks, marsh grasses, piers, and intimate coves enhanced with sculptural features provide a variety of water-edge experiences. Pathways move through tidal grasses and coves, past stabilized gantry towers and piers, which remain as visual benchmarks of the site's industrial past. A sensitive balance of such active and passive recreational opportunities as game courts, ball fields, community gardens, interpretative stations, play areas, café terraces, public art installations, turf amphitheater, and open lawns, reflects the diversity of New York City and the dynamics of its culture of recreation. This diverse landscape has been woven together into a meaningful park environment that draws upon the tradition of Olmsted's Riverside Park to the north.

57

left
**View west from shoreline reveals
Pier I's scalloped edge, winged
shade structure, and light-wand
tower.**

Chelsea Waterfront Park

Project:	**Chelsea Waterside Park**
Location:	11th Avenue to Route 9A—22nd Street to 24th Street
	New York, New York
Start:	Master Plan 1986; Phase I started in 1996, completed in 2000
Client:	New York State Department of Transportation/Route 9A
Design Team:	Thomas Balsley, William Harris, Samuel Lawrence, Steven Tupu,
	Shigeo Kawasaki
Project Team:	Thomas Balsley Associates, landscape architects; Domingo
	Gonzalez Design, lighting; Edwards and Kelsey, civil engineering

left
**Curving walls of color
frame the water-play area
and overlook terrace.**

above
**A "before" view looking west
at 23rd Street**

What began as a pro bono consulting project in 1986 for the Chelsea Waterside Park Association turned into one of Balsley's most creative designs. A vision plan for a park at the foot of 23rd Street evolved into a plan to close the 23rd Street link to Route 9A, thereby capturing a much larger space for a park stretching from 22nd Street to 24th Street that would include a wide range of activities in an area of the city with very little open space. Balsley negotiated the closing of 23rd Street replacing it with a grand promenade—the physical and symbolic link between Chelsea and its waterfront—as the organizing focus of the park. Design considerations depended on such issues as a southern corner that might invite undesirable uses. As a result some unusual, although much desired activities were incorporated, and the southern corner became an adventure dog run, popular with a constituency that uses the park from dawn to midnight.

Balsley listened carefully to a wide range of community desires so that, for example, the promenade passes through a horticultural display area, the only one in the entire Chelsea community. The children's play area is placed near 11th Avenue to insure good visibility. It is separated from a much desired basketball court by an overlook terrace with a comfort station and a concession café that provides parents with a place to sit and have coffee while they watch their children. It also serves as a focus for people from all over the park. What may seem like an overprogrammed park is, in fact, balanced because it fulfills such a range of user desires.

Another difficult process began when Balsley introduced the community to the kinds of materials and design that would assure that the park was designed for "our grandchildren" rather than "our grandfathers." Much of this job of educating and convincing was accomplished by a study of old photographs and illustrations and by

59

Chelsea Waterside Park

Adventure dog run at park's southern tip

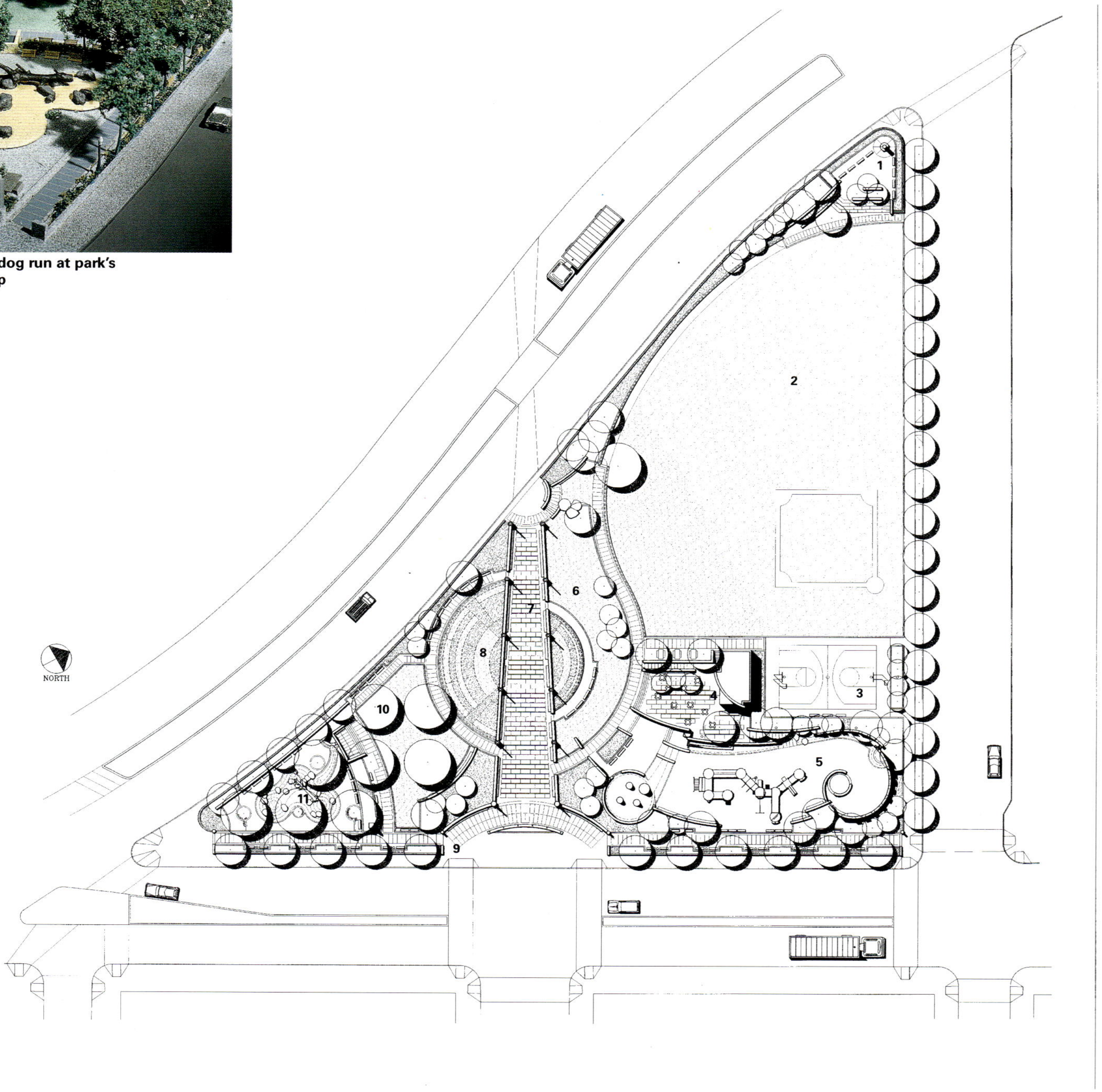

Chelsea Waterside Park Legend

1 Sunset overlook
2 Sports lawn
3 Basketball courts
4 Café terrace
5 Water-play area
6 Picnic lawn
7 Center promenade
8 Garden
9 Entrance pylons
10 Shaded lawn
11 Adventure dog run

NORTH

the clearly expressed idea that the park would reflect the industrial past of the area with the metaphoric use of such materials as large, rough slabs of stone and stainless steel. Many discussions of these issues with members of the community brought about a level of trust that resulted in their granting Balsley a great measure of artistic freedom.

The area north of the center promenade consists of curving paths and forms that provide transition to spaces of active recreation: a sports lawn, for example, and basketball courts, but also an inventive water-play area for children. The southern part of the park with existing trees (it was once a much smaller neighborhood open space, Thomas F. Smith Park) remains available for more passive uses. The park is framed with a distinctive fence, a low wall 18-inches to two-feet high, made of huge slabs of granite with a split-faced finish and a slight batter, on top of which rises a two-and-a-half-foot-high stainless steel fence of welded wire mesh and industrial-looking connections. The 23rd Street entrance to the park has been punctuated with poetic vertical elements, 20-foot-high pylons with floodlights within. Resting on a base

of split-faced stones, the pylons consist of a perforated stainless steel sheet that has been twisted and turned into a column that resembles a tightly rolled banner. Shorter pylons mark the other entrances.

Within the park Balsley has expressed motion in a formalized composition of spiraling, curving forms that are created with walls of different heights. Some walls slip by one another, providing passage between framed spaces. All are painted in colors that are soft but distinctive in the New York landscape. Pavements throughout are large slabs of bluestone or granite bordered by cobblestones, which suggest a narrative that this was once a working waterfront in which original cobblestones have been replaced over the years. In the children's water-play area, multicolored shards resting in pigmented concrete show where water falls or runs.

It is this composition of colorful curving forms, textured pavements, and lush plantings of shrubs, ground covers, flowering trees, and flowers that creates an exciting park as full of activities as of style, a park that will fill the hearts of those who enter it with joy and surprise and a heightened sense of living in the most exciting city in the world.

Entrance pylons detailed in perforated stainless steel on split-faced granite bases mimic furled banners.

Project: **Rockefeller University South Campus**

Location: FDR Drive—64th Street and York Avenue

New York, New York

Dates: Started in 1997, completed in 2000

Client: Rockefeller University

Design Team: Thomas Balsley, Steven Tupu

Project Team: Thomas Balsley Associates, landscape architects; Wendy Joseph,

architect; H. M. Brandston & Partners, Inc., lighting; Weidlinger

Associates, Inc., structural engineering

left
**View across South Campus
garden and overlook plaza with
the Queensboro Bridge beyond**

above
**View of barren plaza before
work began**

right
**Outdoor dining terrace and event
lawn with grove beyond**
Early study for shade structure

An urban oasis with one of the most impressive rosters of Nobel Prize winners of any university in the world, Rockefeller University is a medical research institution with a beautiful campus. Stretching some nine blocks along York Avenue, it includes a 1950s landscape by Dan Kiley. In the late 1970s the campus was enlarged at the southern end by almost seventy percent with three large brutalistic towers. Little or no attention was paid to the landscape.

Two decades later a donor contributed the money for a new landscape to the addition as well as a bridge to a residential area that the university built one block south.

Balsley built on the strengths of the South Campus, its wonderful unobstructed window onto the East River and architectural spacing that allowed sunlight into the area.

The space was also important to the campus, for it was next to the main cafeteria, a gathering place on campus, and a path of travel from the residential component of the university. Its negative aspect was the chopped-up, neglected nature of the space—five different levels!—which begged for a strong unifying element.

First of all, Balsley added a stairway to an elevated plaza in order to incorporate it into the main circulation route of the campus. There he

Rockefeller University
South Campus

placed a small café that could take advantage of the great river view. Another important design move was to create a shade structure that would serve as foreground element to the tall buildings while diverting attention from them. The shade structure took the form of a vortex pointing to the sky. Two smaller plazas at a higher level were simply furnished with benches under trees in distinctive red oval planters. A path detailed by Kiley with white marble, marble chips, and charcoal gray granite provided the inspiration for the paving pattern of the entire space; another quotation from Kiley can be found in an allée of birch trees that provides east-west movement along the north side of the space. Central to the plaza is a circle, its edge articulated by a low polished black granite wall slotted with waterspouts to create a continuous ring of falling water. Balsley's design interventions have created a place of both meeting and contemplation, a haven designed to stimulate and nourish the great scientific minds of the future.

above from left
A ring of water flows over a slotted black granite fountain wall encircling a grove of gingkos.

Stainless steel vortex sculptures provide shade for café seating.

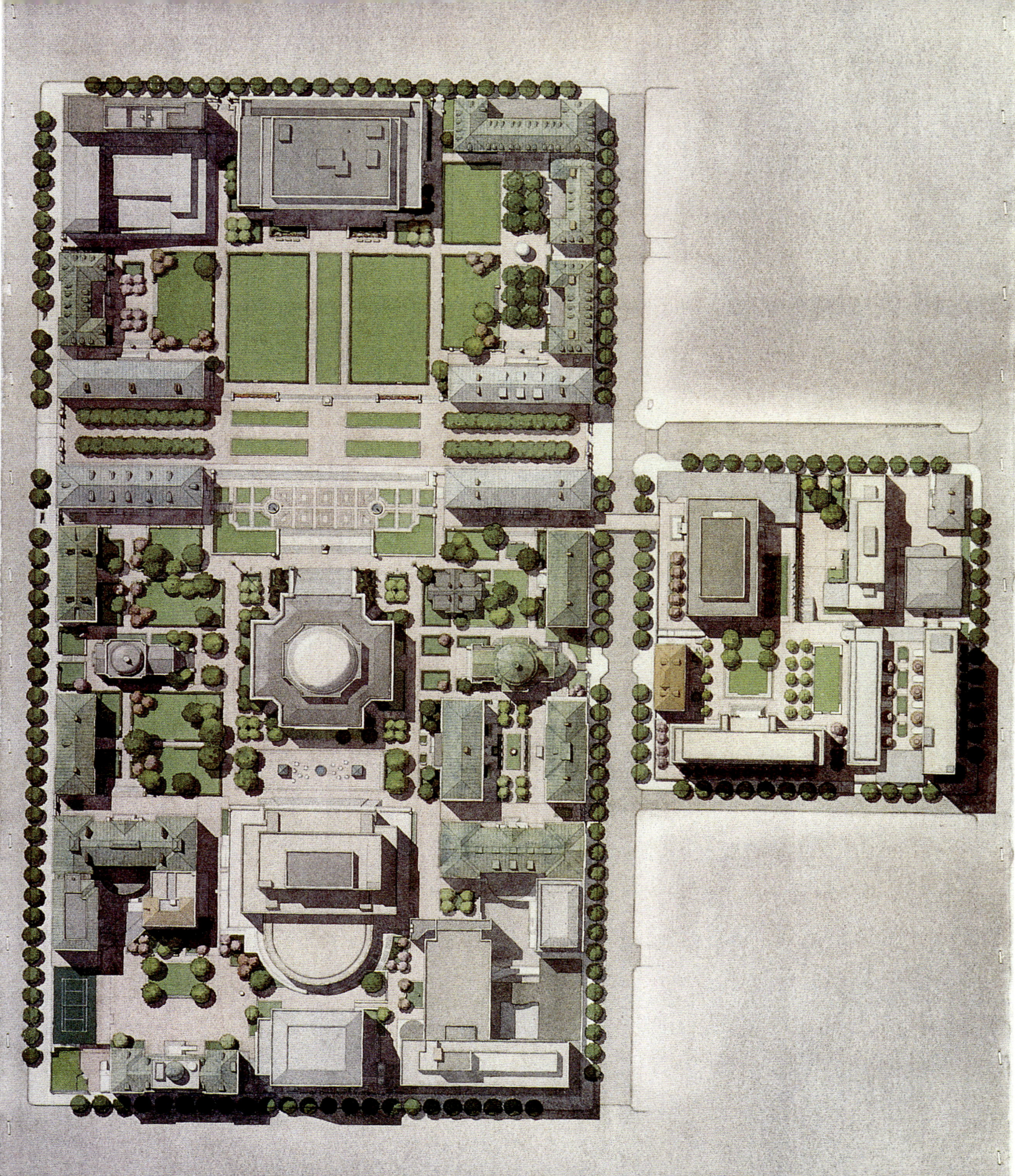

Project: **Columbia University Landscape Master Plan**

Location: 116th Street and Broadway, New York, New York

Dates   Started in 1998, completed in 2000

Client: Columbia University

Design Team: Thomas Balsley, Kathleen Bakewell, William Harris

Project Team: Thomas Balsley Associates, landscape architects; Beyer Blinder Belle,
                   architects; Lynden B. Miller, public garden design; H. M. Brandston &
                   Partners, lighting; Andrew Dolkart, historian

left
**Illustrative landscape
master plan**

The Centennial Landscape Master Plan for Columbia University's historic campus at Morningside Heights provides a long-range vision for the campus environment as well as streetscape guidelines for its surrounding streets. The master plan proposes specific design interventions and guidelines for the campus landscape that are in keeping with its historic character yet responsive to its current and future needs. The work began with extensive historical research into the original plan by McKim, Mead and White and an assessment of current campus conditions and use patterns. The final design proposals address these sometimes conflicting notions by mediating between restoration and the realities of daily campus life. The icons of the original plan—its spatial organization and system of pathways, walls, and stairs—have been preserved while embracing cherished open spaces. Having strayed far from the character of the core historic campus, the harsh north and east campus zones will be transformed gradually into softer landscape quadrangles with shaded lawns and social spaces. The reknitting of the campus landscape will be accomplished with a carefully selected palette of materials for its skeletal system of paving, walls, fences, stairs, hedges, furniture, and lighting, as well as its plantings including flowering trees, ground covers, and the introduction of perennial and annual garden displays. The plan also selects target areas for improvements with detailed designs and cost estimates for each.

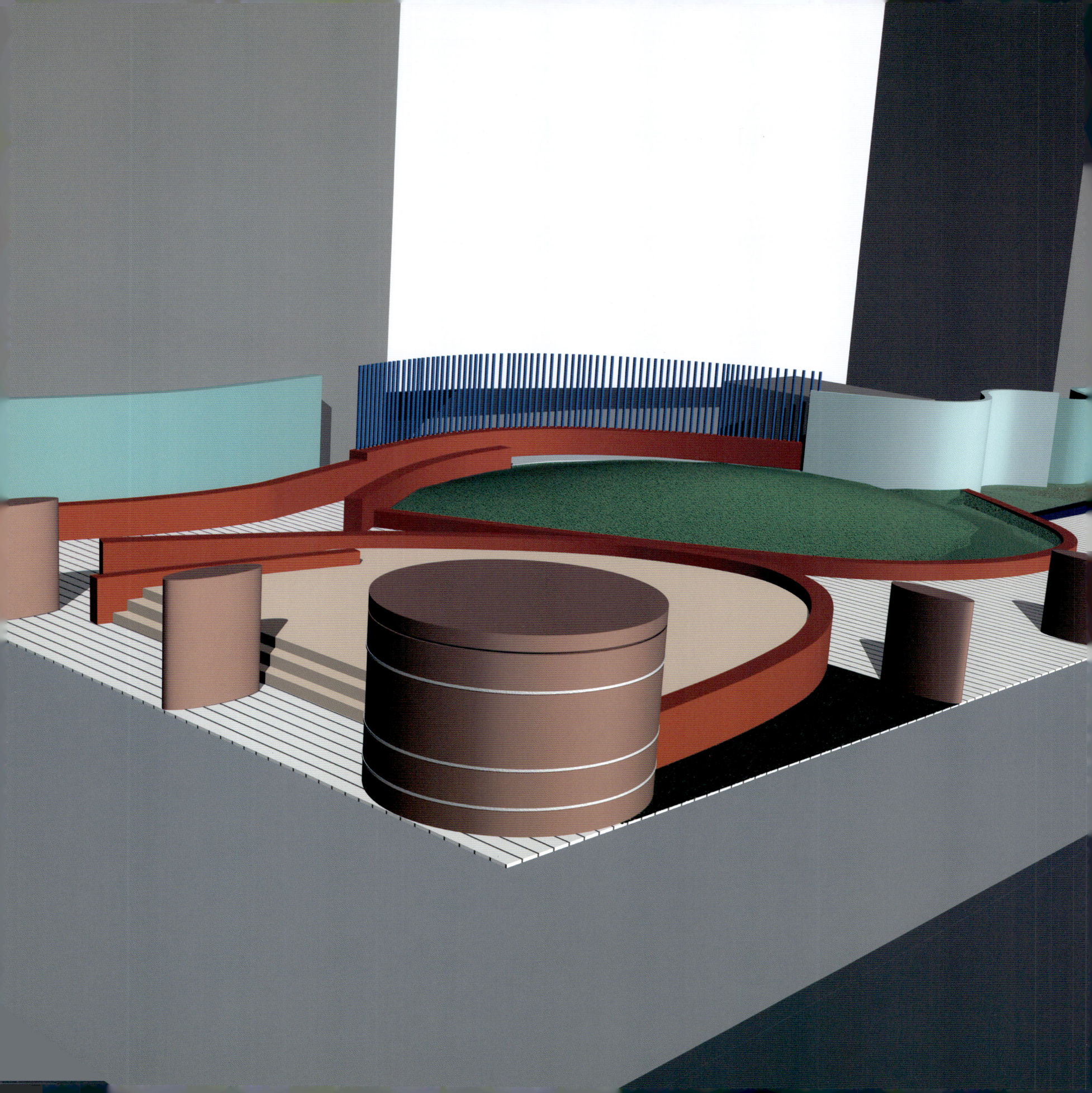

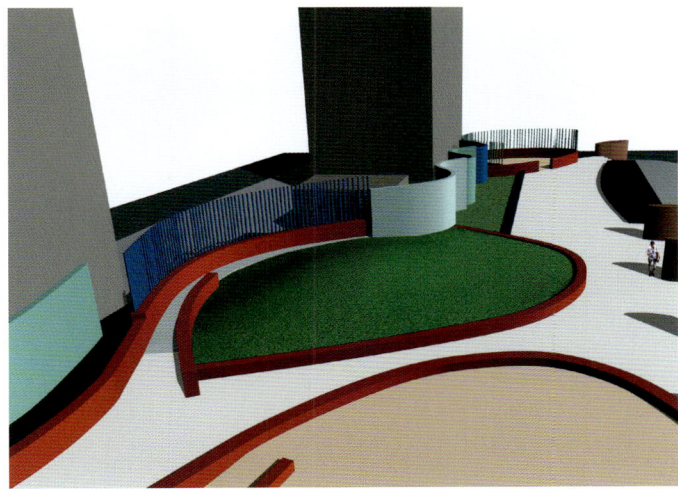

left
**Perspective of corner
café and terrace**

above
**Traverse path
Sloping lawn**

Project:	**Balsley Park**
Location:	9th Avenue—56th Street and 57th Street
	New York, New York
Dates:	Started in 1998, completed in 2000
Client:	Rose Associates
Design Team:	Thomas Balsley, Steven Tupu
Project Team:	Thomas Balsley Associates, landscape architects

Balsley Park, formerly Sheffield Plaza, is located at 9th Avenue between 56th and 57th streets on the West Side. Fifteen years ago it was the only instance in the city in which a bonus plaza was built on a parcel that was not contiguous with the tower receiving the bonus benefits, a practice typically not allowed because the space was removed from the watchful eyes and the security associated with the building. In part because of this, Sheffield Plaza was a failure, attracting vagrants and falling into disrepair. Two attempts to redesign the plaza failed to meet the expectations of the city planning offices and the community board. Finally the client went to Balsley for another try. Balsley listened to the community and perceived that they wanted this space to be more parklike than plazalike. Gaining the trust of his now weary client, he was encouraged to do something artistic that would fulfill community desires while establishing the security of the site.

The plaza was programmed with the idea of building a broad constituency of users: a café kiosk on the most highly exposed corner, a sloping lawn, and a small play area. Security was achieved by building gates that are highly visible during the open hours; these gate-enclosure cabinets also serve as sculptural elements that define the street edge. Most important is a simple diagonal path from 57th Street to 9th Avenue, a desire line for pedestrians who add life and activity—and hence security—to the park from dawn until the wee hours.

Balsley Park

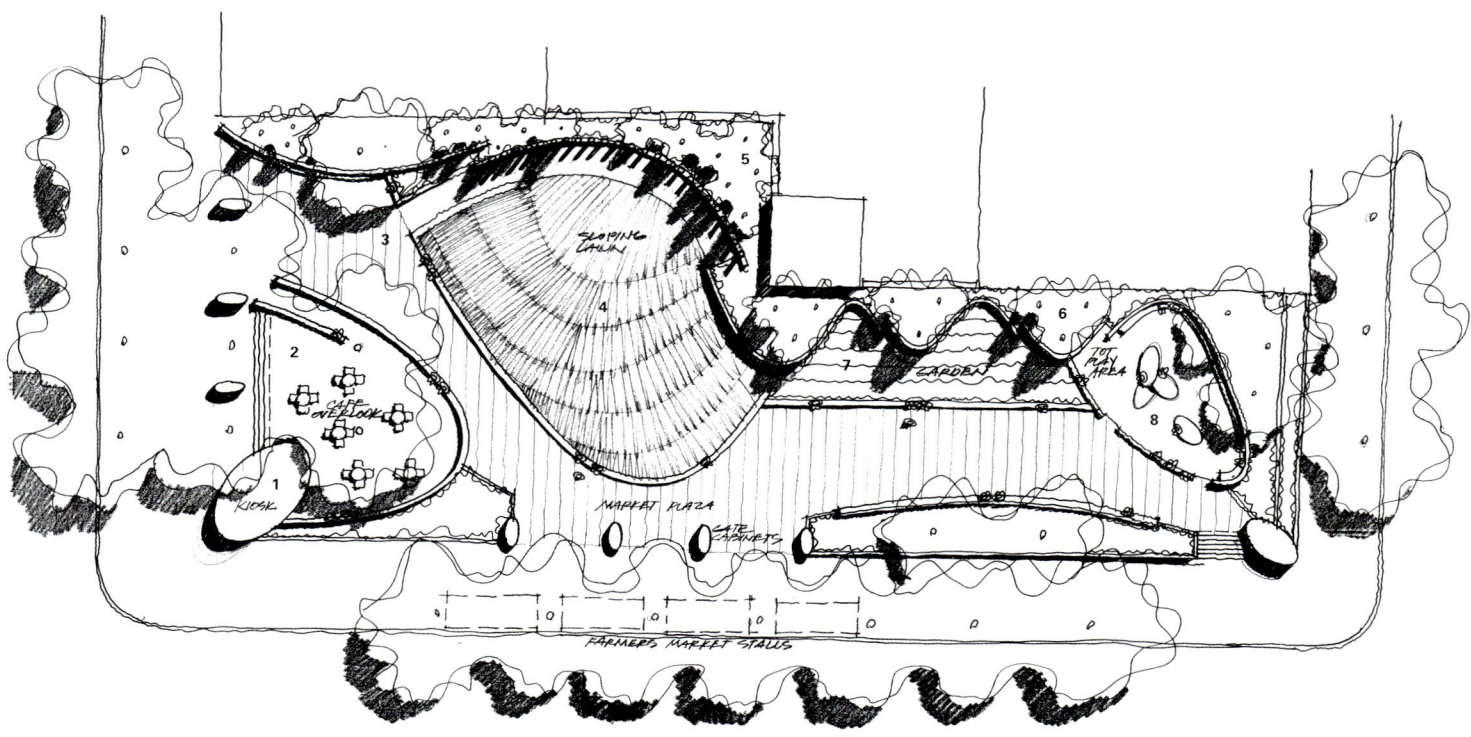

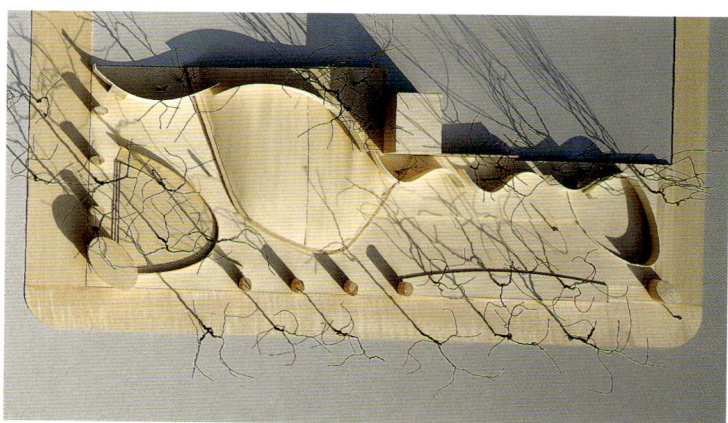

**Balsley Park
Legend**

1 Café kiosk
2 Café terrace
3 Traverse
4 Sloping lawn
5 Pipe walls
6 Ribbon walls
7 Garden
8 Toddler area

left
**Model shows a ground plane
animated with curving forms,
ribbon walls, overlook terrace,
and traverse path.**

The design itself is infused with elements that suggest an escape from the order of the city, from the grid, and from all of the confinements that the human imagination foists upon the urban order. The path ignores the grid, the slope is parklike, and attention is diverted from the walls of the buildings that frame the edge by the creation of a living backdrop of trees. This dense evergreen grove runs the entire length of the park and is fronted by a colorful ribbonlike curving wall that breaks down into a sculptural series of pipes with spaces of five inches or so in between. A counterpoint to the edge of evergreens, this permeable wall clearly shows park users that no dangerous activity is going on behind it. Seatwalls and

walls that edge the terraces are curvilinear and colorful, the curve again destroying the sense of the grid. The kiosk itself is cylindrical in shape, and its associated tables and chairs add another level of comfort while they encourage another user group. The edge along 9th Avenue has been left open to accommodate a green market operation two or three days a week.

In gratitude for Balsley's unusual combination of political savvy, openness to user desires, and imagination in translating those desires into exciting artistic forms, the appreciative client named the new park in Balsley's honor.

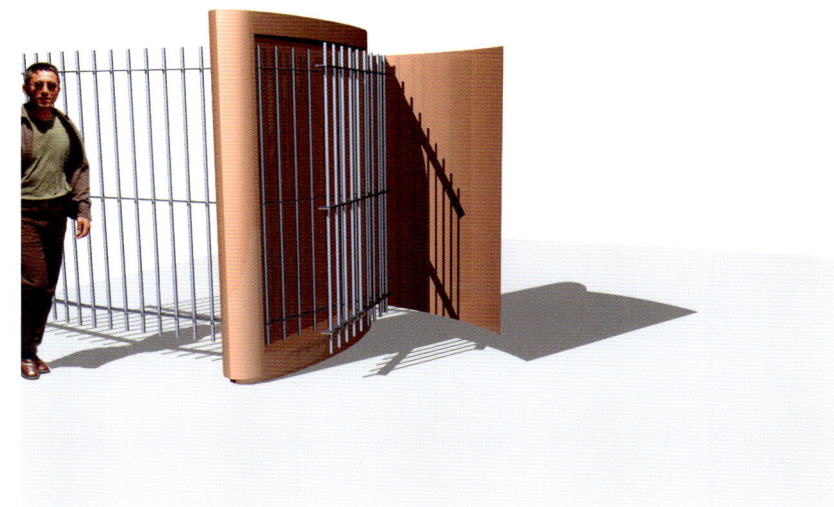

above
Oval gate enclosure

left
Construction fence graphics

Project Time Line

Balsley Associates
1970
Washington Square Park
Play Areas
New York, NY
Fountain Valley Resorts
St. Croix, USVI

1971
Baisley Pond Park
Queens, NY
U.S. Coast Guard Memorial Park
New London, CT

Balsley Balsley Kuhl
1972
Ruppert Housing
New York, NY
Complexe des Jardins
Montreal, Canada

1973
Ruppert Park
New York, NY
Treetops
Hilton Head Island, SC

1974
Pembry Leisure Village
Wales, UK
Applehill Farms
Chappaqua, NY

1975
Westmoor Ecology Park Design
Competition First Prize
West Hartford, CT

1976
Packer Collegiate Institute
Brooklyn, NY

1977
Colonial Plaza
Roanoke, VA
Natural Gas Pipeline Company
Houston, TX

Balsley Kuhl
1978
Cultural Arts Center
Damman, Saudi Arabia
Eckerd Corporate Headquarters
Sarasota, FL
Western Geophysical
Corporation
Houston, TX

1979
Center for Science and Industry
Tampa, FL

Post Oak Center Park
Houston, TX
Fountain Valley Resorts
St. Croix, USVI
Clinton/Hanover Square
Syracuse, NY
Rivergate Community Park
New York, NY

1980
Seafirst Financial Center
Spokane, WA
Tampa City Center
Tampa, FL
Trump Tower Atrium & Terrace
New York, NY
The Atrium
Tampa, FL

Thomas Balsley Associates
1981
Manhattan Place Plaza
New York, NY
Fixed Base Airline Facility
Tampa, FL
Trump Plaza
New York, NY

1982
100 U.N. Plaza
New York, NY
Medgar Evers College
Brooklyn, NY
Cap au Vent
St. Bart, FWI
Reflection Bay
St. Croix, USVI

72

Ruppert Park

Westmoor Ecology Park

Colonial Plaza

Tampa City Center

Manhattan Place Plaza

Treetops

Packer Collegiate Institute

Post Oak Center Park

Trump Tower Waterwall

100 U.N. Plaza

Clinton/Hanover Square

Rivergate Community Park

Cap au Vent

1983

Savoy Plaza and Roof Garden
New York, NY
DeVoe Park
Bronx, NY
Cherokee Sculpture Court
New York, NY
Metropolitan Life Insurance
Campus
Bridgewater, NJ

1984

Centennial Park, Ybor City
Tampa, FL
Juniper Valley Park
Queens, NY
Columbia University East
Campus Courtyard
New York, NY

Normandie Court Plazas
New York, NY
Battery Park City
Buildings B, J, K, and L
New York, NY

1985

East River Esplanade Park
Master Plan
New York, NY
The Rio Plaza
New York, NY
McKinley Park
Brooklyn, NY
Windsor Court
New York, NY
Bristol Plaza
New York, NY
Evans Plaza
New York, NY

The Corinthian Plaza
New York, NY
Black and Decker Regional
Headquarters
Shelton, CT
Queensboro Bridge Open
Space Master Plan
New York, NY
Milford Corporate Center
Milford, CT
Grace Park
New York, NY

1986

Reader's Digest Park
New York, NY
Chelsea Waterside Park
Master Plan
New York, NY

Mathes Residence
Southampton, NY
Shearson Lehman Garden
New York, NY
Paramount Plaza
New York, NY
Bank Street Plaza
White Plains, NY

1987

Penn Station Newark
Urban Streetscape Study
Newark, NJ
Brown University Dormitory
Providence, RI
Castle Hill Park
Bronx, NY
Embassy Suites Hotel
Parsippany, NJ

Port Imperial
Wehawken, NJ
P. O. Byrne Park
Brooklyn, NY
Tribeca Towers Plaza
New York, NY

1988

The Oxford Plaza
New York, NY
Morris Canal Peninsula at
Liberty State Park
Jersey City, NJ
East River Esplanade Park
Phase I
New York, NY
Commonwealth Center
Ashburn, VA
Port Liberté
Bayonne, NJ

Savoy Plaza and Roof Garden

The Rio Plaza

Black and Decker Regional Headquarters

Shearson Lehman Garden

East River Esplanade Park

Metropolitan Life Insurance Campus

Windsor Court

Grace Park

Port Imperial

Morris Canal Peninsula at Liberty State Park

Normandie Court Plazas

The Corinthian Plaza

Queensboro Bridge Open Space Master Plan

1989

Weeping Beech Park
Queens, NY
Purchase Estates
Harrison, NY
Menorah Campus
Buffalo, NY

1990

Shore Road Park Master Plan
Brooklyn, NY
Fordham Plaza
Bronx, NY
Martha Stewart Summer
Residence
East Hampton, NY
Alexander Residence
Amagansett, NY

1991

Downtown Brooklyn
Streetscape Guidelines
Brooklyn, NY
Progressive Insurance
Corporate Headquarters
Cleveland, OH
Hebrew Home for the Aged
Campus
Riverdale, NY

1992

Studio Museum of Harlem
Garden
New York, NY
Riverside South Park
Master Plan
New York, NY

One Penn Plaza
New York, NY
World Trade Center
Osaka, Japan
Cathedral of the Madaleine
Salt Lake City, Utah

1993

NY Coliseum Market Plaza
New York, NY
Performing Arts Center Plaza
Nishinomiya, Japan
Queens West Parks
Master Plan
Long Island City, NY
Hudson River Park Interim
Esplanade
New York, NY

Harlem International
Trade Center
New York, NY

1994

Lincoln Houses Master Plan
New York, NY
Schulweis Residence
Harrison, NY
River Place Community Park
New York, NY
Trump International Hotel &
Tower Plaza
New York, NY
Cohn Residence
Tampa, FL
Hunters Point Community Park
Queens, NY

1995

David's Island
New Rochelle, NY
Garden for the Aged
Riverdale, NY
Martha Stewart Summer Re-
treat, Georgica Pond
East Hampton, NY
Gantry Plaza State Park
Long Island City, NY
Brooklyn Navy Yard Entrances
Brooklyn, NY
Symphony Plaza
New York, NY
Riverside South Park Phase I
New York, NY
Tiffany's Garden
New York, NY

Fordham Plaza

Alexander Residence

Riverside South Park Master Plan

Hunters Point Community Park

Riverside South Park Phase I

Martha Stewart Summer Residence

Downtown Brooklyn Streetscape Guidelines

One Penn Plaza

Gantry Plaza State Park

Tiffany's Garden

Progressive Insurance Corporate Headquarters

World Trade Center Osaka, Japan

Symphony Plaza

NEWSeum

NEWSeum
Arlington, VA
Chelsea Waterside Park Design
Competition, First Prize
New York, NY
888 7th Avenue Plaza
New York, NY
Bridge Plaza
New York, NY
East River Park Pavilion
New York, NY
Seven Springs Golf Resort
Bedford, NY
Hebrew Home for the Aged
Promenade
Riverdale, NY
Waterford Plaza
New York, NY
Hakata Riverain
Fukuoka, Japan

Columbia University
Landscape Master Plan
New York, NY
Onteora Club Master Plan
Sullivan County, NY
Peninsula Park at Queens West
Long Island City, NY

1997
Tahari Ltd. Roof Terrace
New York, NY
Gate City Osaki
Tokyo, Japan
Avalon on the Sounc
New Rochelle, NY
Riverside South Park Phase II
New York, NY
Rivervue
Tuckahoe, NY

Rockefeller University South
Campus Design Competition
First Prize
New York, NY
Chungdong School
Seoul, Korea
Soros Foundation/Open
Society Institute Terrace
New York, NY

1998
Jimbocho Redevelopment
Tokyo, Japan
Grand Central Plaza
New York, NY
Westchester Center
White Plains, NY
La Guardia Airport
Landscape Master Plan
Queens, NY

Madison Belvedere Plaza
New York, NY
Library Green
New Rochelle, NY
Balsley Park
New York, NY
Battery Park City Cinema Plaza
New York, NY
River Park Technology Center
Parsippany, NJ
Harlem on the Hudson
Master Plan
New York, NY
Trump International Plaza
New York, NY
New York Times Capsule
Competition Finalist
New York, NY

1999
Duarte Square
New York, NY
Cohen Pocket-Park
New York, NY
Ferry Point Park
Bronx, NY
Sillerman Courtyard
New York, NY
Avenue of the Americas Plaza
New York, NY
Tudor Investments
Greenwich, CT
Lou Gehrig Plaza
Bronx, NY

Chelsea Waterside Park

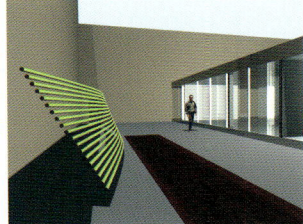
Tahari Ltd. Roof Terrace

**Soros Foundation/Open Society
Institute Terrace**

Library Green

**Harlem on the Hudson
Master Plan**

Hebrew Home for the Aged

Gate City Osaki

Jimbocho Redevelopment

Battery Park City Cinema Plaza

Trump International Plaza

Hakata Riverain

**Rockefeller University South
Campus**

Grand Central Plaza

***New York Times* Capsule
Competition Finalist**

Thomas Balsley
El Paisaje Urbano

Cuando volamos en avion sobre la cuidad de New York parece como si Manhattan podría alcanzar dentro de la palma de una mano. Los edificios parecen ser hechos de barro, curosiamente frágiles. Si no tenemos cuidado podríamos volcar un chapitel. Entre las torres débiles apenas hay espacio para un palillo. Después de aterrizar se cambia el tema. Allí, estas al fondo de una garganta enorme. Los edificios son de hierro y no temen a nadie. De todas formas, por fuera o por dentro, New York siempre parece ser *el lugar,* por eso se considera que cuando la arquitectura paisajista se trasladado a las afueras de la cuidad después de la Segunda Guerra Mundial la profesión abandonó una tremenda oportunidad y un desafío indudable.

En los años 1960 cuando Thomas Balsley se trasladó a New York después de terminar sus estudios universitarios, se encontró con aquel desafío y agarro la oportunidad. Aúnque últimamente a realizado proyectos en otros sitios, en especial Asia, la cuidad de New York es su sede. Tal como New York es un modelo de la cuidad típica norteamericana, y a la vez es única, Balsley también es representantivo de su profesión que a la vez a tenido una trayectoria fuera de lo común. Sus proyectos resaltan. Ejemplos son la torre Trump con una pirámide de arboles sobre un costado del edificio y por dentro una cascada de cinco pisos de altura; o la fuente pirámidal de One Penn Plaza frente al Madison Square Garden que proyecta niebla, o las grúas corredizas gigantescas a las orillas occidentales de rio East. Este último proyecto llamado Queens West es el proyecto que parece probable levantará la fama de Balsley frente al público. Aúnque tener un proyecto que será experimentado por millones de los habitantes de New York no es típico, lo es ser anónimo dentro de su profesión. Millones difrutan de sus labores sin conocer quien es.

Balsley es un hombre guapo y complejo, con las dudas y ánimo, metas y principios que han contribúido a transformar el neuyorquino a figura de novela. Este héroe a veces a aparecido como abogado, financiero, artista, político, a veces arquitecto, pero nunca hasta este momento, un arquitecto paisajista. Balsley no se propone como un hombre de ficción pero su historia de emigración a New York, su lucha para formar su práctica, el desarrollo de su arte y su éxito tiene pertenecia para la comunidad de arquitectos paisajistas que tal vez no sería aparente por razón de su posición única. Aúnque su práctica es en New York, Balsley ha tenido que enfrentar los mismos dilemas entre el arte y la artesanía, el servicio público y la expresión artística que ha contribúido a formar la profesión estos últimos trienta años.

La cuidad de New York no es el único lugar para vivir pero es el lugar donde la gente viene en busqueda del éxito. Sus habitantes comparten la anonimidad en una mezcla cultural y racial. En las palabras de Balsley, "es el cubil del pícaro" y el sitio del enfoque creativo en los Estados Unidos que ofrece oportunidades ricas para los arquitectos paisajistas que buscan desafíos de diseño pero que no teman la diversidad que existe. Estas cualidades, atraeron a Balsley. Fue críado en un pueblo llamado Endicott en el estado de New York pero siempre supo, antes de escojer su profesión, que su destino se encontraba en Manhattan. Cuando era muchacho, su familia mantenía jardines y huertas para uso familiar. Su abuelo paterno había tenido una finca y su abuelo materno, originalmente de Alemania, había trabajado en fábricas

en que se funde y tenía afición de arte. Esta historia familiar formado en fábricas y fincas conformó los ejemplos del desarrollo del joven. Eventualmente, tres de los cinco hermanos Balsley se hicieron arquitectos paisajistas.

Balsley se recuerda un incidente en su colegio que fue indicativo de su carácter y que explica por que escojió la arquitectura paisajista como profesión y también como práctica su profesión. Su padre había sido una estrella de beisbol en la universidad de Syracuse y empujaba a sus hijos a participar en aquel deporte. Balsley tuvo cierto éxito en beisbol pero sin consultar a nadie, cambio a atletismo. Balsley explica esta acción diciendo que, "primero, el beisbol era un deporte de equipo y quería el desafío personal; segundo, no me importaba que atletismo no era considerado con la misma importancia." Esta acción indicaba el conflicto que sentía Balsley entre satisfacer el deseo de complacer a los demás y a la vez despeguarse de los demás. Dice Balsley, "soy rebelde por naturaleza, pero también se que cuando trabajo con otros tengo que escuchar." Estos aspectos contradictories de su persona tal vez han impedido su progreso profesional pero también lo han dado su fuerza.

Balsley a transformado la paradoja de su carácter a su fuerza, combinando las interacciones pragmáticas con idealismo individual, satisfaciendo la colectiva y a la vez proyectando mucho mas, es decir: integrando la responsabilidad social con la expresión artistica. La combinación de diversas posiciones a jugado el papel de mayor importancia en su obra. Al principio, Balsley consideraba su profesión como una extensión de la arquitectura su resultado debido al proceso necesario entre grupos de la comunidad y los promotores de bienes raíces. Balsley a tenido éxito con grupos de la comunidad y a la vez con clientes como Donald Trump, el promotor de gran fama en New York. Ahora, Balsley considera que su papel es intentar comunicar el mismo sentido de responsabilidad a sus clientes y a la comunidad, mesclando esta posición con una visión artistica personal. Balsley siempre escucha y procura mediar, pero últimamente se ha convencido que su responsabilidad como diseñador es guíar la gente mas allá de sus metas concientes para así llegar a una conciencia sobre los espacios e emociónes de mayor significado.

Balsley sigio su vocación y a la vez a su hermano mayor a el programa académico de arquitectura de paisajismo en la SUNY de la universidad de Syracuse. Balsley recuerda que el mensaje central de su educación era el contextualismo, o sea que el arquitecto paisajista tenía que subordinarse al sitio o al contexto. Balsley también fue introducido al modernismo y al concepto, que como él lo explica, "ideas y belleza se pueden expresar sin formas literales." Aqui también descubrio su ínteres en escultura. "Estaba enamorado con el trabajo de Noguchi," recuerda Balsley, "tenía incertidumbre sobre el campo artistico dentro de la arquitectura paisajista, pero estaba fascinado con las posibilidades presentadas por escultura." Su talento y abilidades le ayudaron a recibir muchos honores estudiantiles culminando en 1968 con su ortogación del premio como el mejor alumno.

Por razones económicas, Balsley interrumpía sus estudios cada año para trabajar en la oficina de Glavin y Kotz, donde Jim Gavin le empujaba a desarrollar su talento. Esta etapa de su vida de estudio y práctica ayudo mucho a su formación profesional aúnque también sirvio a aislarle de sus compañeros. Los tres años de experiencia que recibio en esta forma y sus estado económico precario explica por que al recibir su título no sigio su posgraduado pero en vez se lanzo a la práctica. Aúnque tal vez la falta de continuar con sus estudios le dio una desventaja, lanzarse a la práctica le dio confianza como diseñador y le permitio formar una visión de su práctica. En 1968, mientras trabajaba y estudiaba gano de la ASLA premios a la vez como arquitecto paisajista y estudiante, un hecho fuera del lo común. Cuando el tema es su lado pragmático, Balsley da credito a su experiencia con la firma de Currier Andersen y Geda en Hartford, Connecticut. Allí, Charles Currier había tenido mucho éxito económico en su práctica y para el joven Balsley era prueba que alguien podía tener seguridad económica y libertad artistica.

Cuando llego el individualista Balsley a New York no penso en buscar trabajo como empleado de oficina, aúnque su hermano estaba trabajando para M. Paul Friedberg el arquitecto paisajista. Al contrario, Balsley establecio su oficina propia simplemente trabajando desde su cocina. En los próximos años los arquitectos que veían sus croquis y dibujos se quedaban admirados y así consegía trabajo como para mantenerse. Había dificultades en los primeros años. Balsley recuerda que en esos años un arquitecto paisajista no podía adquirir un contrato directo de la cuidad, y que, en sus palabras, "eramos, con la excepción de Friedberg, subordinados a los arquitectos e ingenieros y a las ideas de Robert Moses sobre el uso de diseños uniformes, y de detalles y materiales sin ninguna participación del público".

De importancia mayor a Balsley era el hecho de vivir en New York. Balsley explica que, "hay muchos niveles en New York pero son los subniveles que me interesan aún mas." Aqui Balsley exploraba las escaleras de entrada a las casas, la vida de las calles y de los barrios así aprendiendo de el medioambiente y de sus habitantes. Balsley explica que, "no estudiaba la cuidad desde afuera como muchos otros sino por dentro, viviendo aqui pude estudiar los espacios públicos y el dinámismo en la manera que fueron estudiados por William Whyte en sus estudios fotográficos. Apreciaba cada anaquel, cada apertura era para mi era una prueba." Aprendio rapidamente los símtomas de los espacios públicos que fracasan. Balsley dicen que "parecen desutilizados y vacíos" y en muchos casos habían sido desarrollados por congutos de participantes que no querían permitir actividades afuera de las actividades suyas. Balsley reconocio que los ocupantes de los sitios son aún mas importantes que los sitios propios. "Siempre he tenido interes en diversas culturas y en el dinamismo urbano y en muchos casos me he sentido defraudado por la falta de comprensión de esta diversidad enorme de la cuidad por parte de mis colegas."

El valor de esta experiencia sociológica no se puede sobrevaluar. Ahora, vemos que la percepción de Balsley sobre el diseño de las canchas be baloncesto en el parque de la comunidad de Hunters Point viene de su observación de las interacciones sociales a sus alredededores. En la misma forma, las plazas diseñadas por Balsley en los barrios del Upper East Side comparten vegetación y agua a sus usuarios y también en esa manera el parque de Fordham Plaza permite la presencia de mercados y conciertos espontáneos.

Después de pocos años Balsley tenía dos socios, pero desafortunadamente en ese año, 1973, ocurrio el embargo arabe de petrolio y toda construcción se parálizo en New York. La nueva firma de Balsley Balsley y Kuhl aprovecho la falta de trabajo haciendo muchos trabajos para la comunidad sin recompensa. Viviendo en Greenwich Village, Balsley participaba en muchas reuniones de grupos comunitarios. Dice, "aprendi mucho de el proceso de trabajar en New York, el proceso de revisión publica, las faltas y lo fuerte del sístema. También fomentó amistades que le han servido años después. Esa misma gente ahora esta en posiciones de antiguedad dento de estos grupos." También tuvo contacto con la Comisión de Planificación de la cuidad y poco a poco ellos comezaron a tener confianza en su trabajo. En el aprendizaje de estos procesos, Balsley pulio la abilidad de escuchar y arbitrar, incorporando estas abildades a su trabajo. Aúnque tal vez lo que separa a Balsley de sus colegas es su posición fuerte artística, lo que lo víncula con respeto a su profesión era el aprecio que siente por el dinamismo que viene de la colaboración en la busqueda de un diseño.

Uno de los encantos de Balsley, y que lo haría un buen héroe de ficción, es la abilidad de aprender de sus errores, en especial su aíslamiento de la comunidad de arquitectos paisajistas y la falta de haber ganado aprobación profesional. A la vez de descubrir el processo colaborativo en sus proyectos su aspecto individualista estaba descrubrio un entúsiasmo por su trabajo que no era mutuo en su sociedad profesiónal y aquel situación fracasó. Después de esto, su aíslamiento era mas profundo. Balsley recruerda, "creo que rechazaba la mentalidad de los demás y simplemente quería seguir mi propio camino de diseño y experimentación. Aúnque conocía las fórmulas européas y americanas no tenía ínteres en aplicar aqellas reglas en el diseño de plazas. No creía que eran relevantes a los espacios multiculturales. Nunca solicité premios de la revista Landscape Architecture ni premios de ASLA. Ahora veo que fui muy estrecho en mis ideas." Estos rechazos eran su manera de formular sus téorias y encontrar su propia voz.

Esta forma de pensar parece haber sido importante para poder entender la míopia de la visión de Balsley. Esta autoprotección tal vez lo permitio tener flexibilidad sin vínculos a ningun estilo ni dogma con pura confianza en su abilidad de usar ideas de el clasicismo, el modernismo o el organicismo dependiendo a lo que consideraba lo apropiado. Su crecimiento posacademico ocurrio por medio del descubrimiento y intuición, y su autoprotección le permitio tener un sistema de valores claros. Lo que le mantiene dice Balsley es "la meta primordial a mejorar la vida urbana. Eso es lo que me importa. Ningun premio ni reconocimiento profesiónal pude reemplazar el orgullo y satisfacción que siento cuando camino por mis obras, llenas de gente de todas partes. Juzgo el éxito de los espacios públicos no por los premios si no por si son queridos por el pueblo." De todas maneras, Balsley reconoce la gente que le ha influenciado como William Whyte, John Ormsbee Simonds, Hideo Sasaki, y Karl Linn; en diseño, Paul Friedberg, Dan Kiley, Lawrence Halprin, Isamu Noguchi, Peter Walker y los diseñadores catalanes de los años 1980.

Eventualmente el momento de Balsley llegó. El dice, "no se si puedo explicar cuando fue pero los promotores de bienes raices de New York me descubrieron.

Consegui mucho trabajo por que les escuchaba. No les decía lo que querían oír para simplemente hacer lo que yo quería con la única meta de conseguir premios." Balsley entendía las metas de ellos y de las comunidad y demonstaba como unir las dos, un hecho de mayor dificultad en la cuidad New York.

Las oportunidades para trabajar en proyectos con financiamiento privado vinieron a Balsley con proyectos como el parque de la esplanada del East River, una intervención dictada por leyes sobre el impacto ambiental y el código sobre las plazas de "bonus" que resultaron de las leyes sobre la zonificación de los años 1960 cuando la cuidad decidió intercambiar mayor altura en el deseño de rascacielos con plazas de espacios abierto a sus bases. Estas plazas tenían que conformar a un codigo administrado por el Departamento de Planificacción. Segun Balsley, los codigos originales resultaron en espacios vacíos que solo permitían el retiro de propiedad hasta un futuro cuando los promotores podían cambiar la ley y presentar otros diseños reintegrando esta propiedad vacía. Con tiempo, el codigo fue modificado para ser mas estricta con respeto al acceso y servicicos en esta forma dando respaldo a los diseños de Balsley.

Trabajando en una cuidad con poca esperanza de aumentar sus espacios abiertos, Balsley fue uno de los pocos arquitectos paisajistas que vieron las oportunidades de aquellos espacios y sus oportunidades en diseño. Por razón que los promotores ganaban mucho dinero en sus obras con los aumnetos de area, los presupuestos de estas plazas rara vez presentaban problema. "Si quieren reducir el presupuesto o disminuír los servicios, simplemente les indico el codigo," dice Balsley; "los promotores saben que un parque o plaza bien diseñada es una ganancia para la cuidad y si es bien mantenida aumenta el valor de la propiedad. Estoy en los ceilos por que al la vez sirvo al cliente, empleando un buen presupuesto, y también al público. Todos ganamos."

En solo un año Balsley diseñó trece plazas y ahora tiene mas que trienta por Manhattan. La crítica que Balsley tiene de algunas de sus obras es que les considera muy contextual." Creo que mi definición del contextualismo era muy estrecho y literal. Pero si en estas plazas hay una falta de personalidad, por lo menos satisfacen los requisitos del público. A veces algunos de los espacios refieren demaiado a sus edificios vecinos que parecen ser espacios privados. Manhattan Plaza, 100 U. N. Plaza y Shearson Lehman Garden todos tienen este aspecto pero en cierto sentido son éxitos como retiros urbanos. Estos espacios manifiestan la idea de la naturaleza dento de la cultura de la cuidad. Usan vegetación, agua y piedras en diseños complicados para créar espacios tranquilos. La buena noticia de todo esto es que Balsley ha sido contratado a remodelar las plazas de los años 1960 como la plaza del General Motors Building, la Paramount Plaza, y la Sheffield Plaza aquel nombre que sera cambiado a Balsley Park en reconocimiento de la contribución de Balsley a la cuidad. Todas estos diseños reflejan la dirección de Balsley a hacer espacios públicos y tal vez tendran acogido con otros arquitectos paisajistas que le siguen.

Balsley recuerda su epifanía profesional a visitar Barcelona en 1987. Allí observó las obras que se hacia para la olimpiadas de 1992. Explica Balsley que dado su experiencia en New York, "me quede admirado que una cuidad con una historia tan profunda podía hacer ese salto al siglo 21 con su diseño." Segun Balsley, el alcalde de aquel cuidad, Pasqual Maragall y el planificador, Oriol Bohiras "desarrollaron todo un sistema de calles, parques y plazas en la cuidad que eran todo que soñaba y quería hacer en New York." En aquel ambiente, Balsley veía expresiónes de el espíritu humano que inspiraban, espacios de orden y composición moderna con espontaniedad inspiradas por el arte y diseño catalan. En vez de bloquear el diseño progresista, los lideres de la cuidad lo habían obligado asi facilitando el proceso.

Balsley se quedo admirado con la base cultural de aquel obras. Dice, "la filosofía catalan mezcla el sentido común con la absurda locura de la creación artistica." Para Balsley esta experiencia transformó su personalidad y su diseño. Dice, "me siento catalan." La idea de diseño que resultó en Catalonia no era el resultado de una sola expresión artistica, ni de un individuo, sino de ideas tratando de satisfacer el acuerdo con el pueblo. Barcelona para él fue la prueba que el arquitecto paisajista puede combinar arte y su conciencia para créar un diseño social.

Los diseños mas advertidos de Balsley en los años 1980 también resultaron en parte por que por la primera vez en su vida se sentía seguro económicamente. Siempre su meta había sido sobrevivir económicamente. Después de la caída de la bolsa en 1997 la exigencia le empujó a tener otra perspectiva. Dice, "si no voy a ser rico por que no usar la energía negativa de mi vocación artística y la experiencia en diseño que he desarrollado en estos últimos quince años?"

Esta transformación ocurrio mientras recibía proyectos de mayor importancia. Algunas de ellas eran en Japon. Ejemplos son El World Trade Center en Osaka y la Gate City en Tokyo, este último un proyecto que acomodaba cuatro esculturas de Balsley. Sin embargo, la mayoría de sus proyectos han sido en New York formando parte del movimiento en los Estados Unidos a rescatar sus centros y sus malecones abandonados. En este tiempo Balsley a diseñado algunos de los parques mas significativos de New York. Su nueva dirección mas experimental se manifiesta en obras como el Esplanade Park (aquel obra a progresado durante los últimos once años), Chelsea Waterside Park, Gantry Plaza State Park y el campus sureño de Rockefeller University.

En su proyecto para Gantry Plaza, los materiales cambían cuando uno se acerca al agua, comenzando con finos y pulidos a la entrada a los mas crudos por las orillas. Esto refleja una filósofia fuera de lo relacionado al contexto. En un artículo en el New York Times, Herbert Muschamp escribió que Gantry Plaza eran un espacio "especial que manifestaba la mano del diseñador. Por que Balsley se ha permitido entrar a lo que Gaston Bachelard llamaba 'la poesia del espacio' o sea un mundo de imagenes, relaciónes, descubrimiento y sorpresa. Lo pequeño, la miniatura, la inmensidad intima en una dialéctica de afuera y de adentro. Estas son los conceptos de Bachelard. Uno los siento aqui en un profusión de formas."

La última decada de trabajo para Balsley ha sido con convicción que el contextualismo y el tradiciónalismo han sido ciegamente seguidas. Dice Balsley, "A pesar de la reputación de New York como el centro global del arte y de la creatividad, los edificios y espacios manifiestan haber sido productos de un proceso muy conservador aúnque bien intencionado que ha aplastado idéas nuevas e inovativas resultando en lo mediocre. En la busqueda de un acuerdo general y en un vacío de prototipos alternativos éxitosos, los burócrates de la cuidad han respaldado lo mas seguro que en muchos casos ha sido copías débiles de la arquitectura paisajista del siglo 19 usando como modelo el Central Park. Con la excepción de ciertos diseñadores de fuera que pueden arriesgiar más, no hay apoyo en la cuidad para los diseñadores que quieren ser diferentes. En muchos casos son exilados a la 'Siberia' del los diseñadores." Esta atitude choca con lo que Balsley piensa es la meta mas importante de su trabajo y eso es dar un significado al espacio que viene de su relevancia y su cultura y tendra relevancia a generaciónes futuras. Los espacios deberían tener la abilidad de enfrentar el espírito humano y inspirarlo mas allá de los limites de la imaginación. La responsibilidad es mas que la acomodación al medio ambiente presente.

Balsley se opone al uso de forma sin sentido. Dice, 'mi trabajo responde al ser humano, su voz interior que habla de lo justo. Mi trabajo necesita compartir y tener sentido. Creo que el espacio público es sagrado y tenemos la obligación de mantener ese espacio. Es el campo para el intercambio de idéas democráticas que permiten la mezcla de las diferentes classes sociales, culturales y económicas. Allí es el desafío mayor. El éxito de un proyecto depende en la consideración de su uso por la mas grande variedad de gente. Diseñadores tienen que escuchar a todas estas gentes que son usuarios del espacio, los dueños de perros, los que patinan, no se puede considerar el espacio como adorno.

Mezclado con su convicciónes programáticas y sociales es lo que Balsley describe como "el instante cuando necesitamos cosas que nos despiertan, nos incomodan, nos hace sentir que tenemos espíritu." Usando interpretaciónes metáforicas o iconóclasticas su trabajo refleja nuestros imagines culturales. Dice,"siempre estoy explorando nuevas formas que reciben formas vernaculares del medio ambiente urbano. Pero si el trabajo tiene que ser juzgado tiene que decir algo y darnos respuestas. Por ejemplo: de que epoca es este sitio?" Balsley tiene muchas ideas que quiere manifestar, por ejemplo el uso de los avances tecnólogicas de comunicacción de video. Aunque la televisión y el internet han contribuido al declive de las reuniones públicas, la pantalla de video puede ser usada como un icono cultural para atraer la vida a los espacios abandonados en la manera que el malabarista de Holly Whyte que fisicamente atabia a personas desconocidas unos a otros. Balsley nos hacer recuerdor que a veces el desafío mayor del diseñdor es controlar el ego personal para así poder permitir que la energía de la cuidad se exprese a si misma. Dice, "trato de crér escenarios de teatro para el medio ambiente urbano, espacios que son acojedores y que invitan la experimentación y apoyan la idea de vivir muchas vidas, despegando de la agenda."

El imagen del escenario parece ser clave de la filosofía de Balsley por varias razones. La primera es la cuestión de su proceso. Balsley insiste en la importancia del proceso de recibir la aprobación del publico, un primer acto del público en todo el proceso. Dice, "conceptos de diseño no vienen de diagramas. La mezcla y desarrollo vienen de por adentro. El proceso público tiene que tener campo para expresión, y contracción, como una gelatina que absorbe, empuja. jala pero aún mantiene su

idea basica. Este proceso no es de compromisos sino viene de la necesidad de preservar el concepto del diseñador frente a las necesidades del público. En circunstancias ideales el diseñador tiene el papel de director tratando de asegurar la realización de la obra y a la vez manteniendo las ideas conceptuales." Como diseñador intuitivo, Balsley a desarrollado un proceso creativo que depende sobre el síntesis del programa y del sitio, una "sopa" que acoge conceptos, expresiónes de forma, y también colaboraciónes públicas y con otros profesiónales y artistas y con cómites del público.

La segunda manera en cual el imagen del escenario es apropiado en la obra de Balsley nueva y vieja es que aparte de su fuerza particular las piezas individuales se integran. Aunque séan las esculturas de Cuidad Entrada en Osaka, las "tonterías" en los muelles de Gantry Plaza State Park o las bancas en forma de olas, cada elemento transforma al espectador a un actor en su obra. En su obra vemos una matriz formal dentro que formas y objetos son yuxtaposiciónados a veces en harmonía a veces al punto entre lo orgánico y lo formal, lo construído y lo natural, la trama y la sorpresa, *sena* y *rauxa*. Vemos el síntesis de la meta social, las necesidades del cliente y la expresión artística en una integración de arte con sentido al ambiente urbano, una tranformación del compartamento humano que esta al fondo del corazon de Balsley. Dice, "la mayoria de los arquitectos paisajistas estan ciegos al impacto enorme que tenemos sobre millones de vidas."

Tomando estas palabras en mente miramos hacia New York con una nueva visión. Cuando miramos hacia la cuidad desde el aire vemos dentro de todo que parece frágil el verde del Central Park, la obra maestra del siglo 19. Dentro de la cuidad arodeada por edificios a veces ni vemos un pedazo de verde, y cuando lo vemos casi siempre se nota la influencia de, aúnque realizado en forma débil, la obra de Frederick Law Olmsted. Tal vez necesitamos ver la falta de espacio verde y el pasado como pruebas que hay caminos que nos espera como arquitectos paisajistas contemporáneos. Lo que Balsley llama "el campo social de una sociedad urbana enérgica." Se realizerá estos sitios? Como seran? Seran diseñados en manera conservadora o seran creádas para los rascaceilos y calles que continuan a hacer esta cuidad "*el lugar*" para el siglo 21?

Podemos ser optimistas sobre el futuro. Balsley ha estado dejando sus huellas sobre New York desde 1969 y su carerra esta apenas comenzando. Su próximo escenario urbano tal vez esta a la vuelta de donde sentamos y estamos seguros que aquel espacio hablará al futuro y no a un pasado cansado. Balsley a encontrado su propia voz pero por que representa lo mejor de su profesión hay esperanza que otros arquitectos paisajistas tomarán sus propios pasos intrepidos en la dirección del arte.

トーマス・ボーズリーの
アーバン・ランドスケープ

ニューヨーク市上空を飛行機から見下ろすと、マンハッタンは手のひらの中にすっぽりと収まりそうだ。建物群は粘土でできている様に見えて面白いぐらいに壊れやすそうである。注意深く操縦しないとうっかり尖塔にぶつかって折ってしまうかもしれない。これらのもろい塔と塔の間には爪楊枝が入るか入らないかぐらいの.隙間しかない。これを地上から見ると状況は実に全く別である。今度は壮大な渓谷の底に立っているかのようである。建物は鉄でできていて、我々をものともしない。たしかにニューヨークは上空や内側や周辺のどこから見ても「そうあるべき場所」に見えるのだが、その一方、第二次世界大戦後にランドスケープ・アーキテクチャーの活動の場が都市の郊外へ移動した時、同市には巨大な機会と同時に否定しがたいチャレンジが残されたと言える。

学部を卒業して1960年代末にニューヨークに移り住んだ時、トーマス・ボーズリーはそのチャレンジと機会の両方に出くわした。近年になってボーズリーは世界の他の地域、特に極東でのプロジェクトに携わってきたが、ニューヨークは依然として彼の拠点である。この都市がアメリカにある他の多くの都市の単なる一つの巨大な例でありながら、なおかつユニークであるのと同様に、ボーズリーは現代のランドスケープ・アーキテクトたちを代表していながら、その作品は普通とは違った方向に変化してきた。ボーズリーの作品はいたるところに見受けられる。例えば、トランプタワーの角のピラミッド状に植え込まれた木々や、その屋内にある五階の高さから落ちる滝、マディソンスクェアーガーデンの真向かいにあるワン・ペンプラザとそこにある霧を吹き出すピラミッド状のグラナイト彫刻、もしくは、イーストリバーの西側に聳え立ついくつかのガントリーなどが挙げられる。しかしながら、これらのガントリーがあるが故に際立っているクィーンズ・ウエストでのプロジェクトこそが、今後彼の名前を公共のレヴェルにまで高めそうである。もし、その作品が毎日数百万人のニューヨーカーたちによって経験されているがゆえにボーズリーを普通でないと捉えたとしても、彼の置かれた状況は他のほとんどのランドスケープ・アーキテクトたちとたいして変わりはない。つまり、数百万人が彼のいくつかのプロジェクトを見たり経験したりしていても、彼らはボーズリーの名前を全く知らないのである。

ボーズリーは器用でありながら複雑な人物で、自己懐疑心を持ち、自信、究極目的、そしてある種のタイプのニューヨーカーたちを数百もの小説のヒーローに仕立てあげたいくつかの行動原理といったものを兼ね備えている。そうしたヒーローたちは往々にして弁護士や資本家や政治家であったり、時には建築家であったりするのだが、今日までそれがランドスケープ・アーキテクトであった例はない。トム・ボーズリーは決して自分自身をあたかも小説のヒーローであるかのように見せたりはしないが、ニューヨークに来て、生きる術を学び、事務所を運営し、技を磨き、そして数百万の人々が楽しむ公共空間をデザインしているという彼の経歴は、そのユニークな背景が一見では露呈しないという点でランドスケープ・アーキテクチャーのコミュニティーに良く当てはまる。ニューヨークという大きな鍋の中で、工芸対美術、公共へのサービス対自己表現といった過去三十年にわたってこの職業に影響を及ぼしてきた対立概念のジレンマに、ボーズリーも立ち向かわなければならなかった。

ニューヨークは単に「そうあるべき場所」なのではなく、人々がやってきて成功する、つまり自分自身を試す場所でもある。そこは匿名性と文化的人種的多様性を提供するが、それはボーズリーの言葉によれば「ならず者の隠れ家」であり、デザインのチャレンジを渇望し逆境を恐れないランドスケープ・アーキテクトにとって、豊かな機会を提供する、アメリカの創造性が最も結集した場所である。ボーズリーはニューヨークが持つこれらの全ての性質に魅了された。アイビーエムの拠点と多くの靴工場がある、ニューヨーク州はエンディコットという小さな町で成長した彼は、将来何になるかを決めるよりずっと以前に、自分が将来ニューヨークへ行くことだけはわかっていたと言う。ボーズリーの成長期には、彼の家族は庭と果樹園を自分たちで使うために保有していた。彼の父方の祖父は農業を営んでおり、他方ドイツからの移民である母方の祖父は鋳物工場で働き、趣味でアーティストであり、ボーズリーにとって素材や絵画のレッスンの源であり、芸術的探求のモデルであった。工場と農場というバックグラウンドは共に、物を作るという良い例を提供した。結果的にボーズリー家の五人の子供のうち三人がランドスケープ・アーキテクトになった。

ボーズリーは高校で起きたある出来事を、彼の性格と職業の選択の理由として挙げる。この話は第三者にとっては、彼がその職業にどの様に従事してきたかをも明らかにするものである。彼の父親はシラキュース大学で野球のスター選手であったが、それゆえ子供たちにスポーツをすることを勧めた。ボーズリーは集団で行うスポーツに秀でていて、それは高校での彼の人気を保証した。しかし突然、彼は父親との相談もなしに野球をやめてクロスカントリーと陸上競技を始めた。「二つのことが起きていた。まず最初に、それらは集団スポーツではなかった。私は自分の行動だけで事の成り行きを決めたかった。次に、両方とも観衆には全く人気のないスポーツであった。だれも陸上競技会で誰が勝ったか気に留めなかった」とボーズリーは言う。ここで我々は第三の点を挙げることが出来る。つまり、他の人を楽しませたいという実際的な欲求と著しい個人主義との間の衝突である。「私の性格は非常に反抗的なのだが、その反面十分実際的で、もし他の人のためになにかを建てるとしたら、彼らの言うことに耳を傾けなければならないのだということも知っている」とボーズリーは認める。このような反抗的で個人主義的な傾向の故に彼の人格形成がやや遅くなったかもしれないが、それらはまた彼の強みにもなった。

社会における責任と自己表現とをうまく融合させながら、他の人々と実際的に協力しつつ個人の理想を追求し、その協力者たちのグループを満足させながらその先へと進む。そうすることによってボーズリーは彼の矛盾した性格を利点に転換してきた。そしてこの融合は彼のキャリアにおいて大きな役割を果たし、それは彼のデザインに現われている。初めは、ランドスケープ・アーキテクチャーは建築の延長であり、近隣との話し合いや施主の意向を反映させる社会的プロセスを経て産み出されると理解していた。彼はコミュニティーグループもドナルド・トランプのような個人も上手く対処してきた。しかし今日の彼が考えるランドスケープ・アーキテクトの役割は、この「施主と公共を両方を満足させる責任」が「芸術的表現というもっと個人主義的な視点」と組合わさったものとなっている。ボーズリーはいつも人の話を聞き、対立意見を調停してきた。しかし過去十年、「デザイナーの責任とは、人々が意識するプロジェクトのゴールを越えてそれより深く重要な空間や感情へと彼らを導くことである」という確信を持って、今度は彼自身の内なる声にも耳を傾けてきた。

ボーズリーは彼の芸術的欲求のままに彼の兄、ジムの後を追ってニューヨーク州立大学の一つであるシラキュース大学でランドスケープ・アーキテクチャーを.専攻した。彼は自分の受けた教育の根幹は、ランドスケープ・アーキテクチャーはその敷地と建築のコンテクストに従属するものであり、ランドスケープは建築の延長であると主張するコンテクスチャリズム(contextualism)であったと記憶している。そこでボーズリーは、モダニズムと、「アイデアと美はいわゆる形態が無くても表現可能である」という概念を教えられた。彼が彫刻をしたいという欲求を見いだしたのもシラキュースにおいてであった。ボーズリーは回想して言う。「私は早い時期からノグチに心酔していた。ランドスケープ・アーキテクチャーの領域を自由に歩きまわる彼の芸術的柔軟性に複雑な気持を持っていた。しかし私は、彫刻とランドスケープとの融合によって呈示された数々の可能性に魅了された。それは私にとってサイト・アートとの初めての出会いであった。」ドローイングとデザインに優れた彼は、数々のデザイン優秀賞を得て、1968年にはOutstanding Senior Awardを得た。

経済的理由で、毎年ボーズリーは大学へ行くのを中断してグレーブン・アンド・コッツのランドスケープ・アーキテクチャー事務所で働かなければならなかった。ボーズリーは、この仕事による大学教育の中断で、幸いにもランドスーケープの教育という点では良い経験をしたが、彼は周囲のクラスメートたちから孤立してしまった。彼の緊迫した経済状況に加えて、こうして彼が得た実際的なデザインの経験からして、彼がなぜ大学院に進まなかったかが理解できる。彼はもうなす術を心得ていたのである。たとえあるレヴェルにおいて、大学院に行かないことは損失であったとしても、すぐに社会に飛び出したことで彼のデザイナーとしての自信は確固としたものとなり、彼の持つ実践的なランドスケープ・アーキテクチャーの視点はユニークに形成された。(ボーズリーが勉強しながら働くことによって、1968には数々のASLA賞に印象深い結果が起こった。その年彼は、プロフェッショナルのための賞と学生のための賞をひとつずつ勝ち取ったのである。)ボーズリー

は自分の実践的側面を語るとき、コネティカット州ハートフォードにあるクーリエ・アンダーソン・アンド・ジーダの事務所で働いた数年を重要な経験として認める。チャールズ・クーリエは大きく且つ成功した事務所を財政的に上手く経営していた。これは野望に満ちたボーズリーにとって、財政的安定と芸術表現の自由は両立するのであって対立するものではないということの頼もしい証拠であった。

独立心旺盛なボーズリーは、ニューヨークに移住して来たとき、彼の兄がM.ポール・フリードバーグの事務所で働いていたにもかかわらず、他人の事務所で働くことを考えなかった。彼の回想によれば、そのかわりT定規を食卓テーブルに据えることによって自分の事務所を始めた。その後数年間、彼のスケッチとレンダリングを見た建築家たちがそれらを気に入り、忙しくするのに十分な数のプロジェクトを依頼した。しかしある意味で、ニューヨークでの最初の数年は息が詰まるようであった。「ランドスケープ・アーキテクトたちはニューヨーク市当局と直接コンタクトを取ることが法律上許されていなかった。我々は建築家やエンジニアたちに従属していて、フリードバーグを除いて、時代遅れのランドスケープ・アーキテクチャーの番人とでも言うべきロバート・モーゼスの提唱する規格化されたデザイン、ディテール、マテリアルといった、殆んど公共の意向を無視したアイデアに影響されていた。」

ボーズリーのキャリアーにとって最も大切なことは、彼がニューヨークでの生活経験を実際に生かしているという事である。「ニューヨークは多くの異なるものが積層していて、私は下に隠れている層に、より深い興味を覚える。」彼は、建物の玄関口や通りの人々の活動、そして多くの近隣を歩きまわりながら、彼が働くことになるであろう地域の環境や、将来空間デザインを提供することになる人々について理解していく。「私は都市を単に離れた位置から理解しようとせず、実際にそこに住んだ。ちょうどフリードバーグが行政官たちとではなく子供たちと遊ぶことによって解答を見いだしたように、私は公共のオープンスペースとそこでの活動を、ウィリアム・ホワイトの露出の長い写真作品のようなやり方で調査した。小さな窓の棚や窓そのものの一つ一つが私の実験場であった。」彼は失敗しているいくつかのパブリックスペースの現象についてすばやく学んだ。それらは「注意を向けられることなく且つ味気なく」、限られた地元の人々によって運営されていて、彼等のそこでの活動が、より多様な活動の可能性を妨げているのだった。その場所を利用する人々について調査することは、その場所そのものの形質について調べることと同じくらい重要であるとボーズリーは理解した。「私はいつも文化的多様性と都市活動に興味を持ってきた。そして、都市内のオープンスペースを利用する巨大な数の多様な人々を理解したり彼等の意向を取り入れたりすることには全く興味を示さない私の仲間たちに対して、しばしば失望してきた。」

このボーズリーの社会学的デザインの過程をいかに高く評価しても評価しすぎることはない。ハンタースポイント・コミュニティーパークにあるバスケットボールコートはニューヨーク市民によるユニークなコートサイドでの共同体的活動のためにデザインされ、アッパーイーストサイドにあるいくつかのプラザは近隣の住民に非常に尊重される水と緑をもたらし、そしてフォーダムプラザのレイアウトは即興的に繰り広げられるマーケットと音楽のためのステージセットを提供している。今日、我々はボーズリによるこうした認識の成果を目の当たりにするのである。

この都市で数年間活動した後、彼は二人のビジネスパートナーを得た。残念なことに1973年は「アラブ産石油が輸入禁止になりニューヨークの全ての建設クレーンが姿を消した」年であった。しかし、この経済的スランプはボーズリーのキャリアにとって要の出来事となった。なぜなら収入を約束する契約が全くなく、この新しい事務所においてボーズリーとクールは報酬のない仕事をした。グリニッジビレッジに、そして後にユニオンスクエアのそばに住んで、ボーズリーは多くのコミュニティー役員会や近隣住民のミーティングに出かけた。「私はニューヨーク市のユニークな公開審査の過程、その利点と欠点を学んだ。そしてそこで人々と良い関係を築き上げた。二十五年前に一緒に仕事をした人々が、今やコミュニティー役員会の年長格のメンバーになっていたりする。彼はニューヨーク市の都市計画委員会、そこでのスタッフや評議会のメンバーたちを知るようにも

なった。コンセンサスがいかに作られるかを知ることによって、人々の言うことに耳を傾け、意見の調整をし、それをデザインに転化する術を学んだ。近年になってその強いアーティスティックな欲求のためにボーズリーは大衆から遠ざかってきたかもしれないが、今でも彼が最重要視するのは、人々の要求に最も良く答えるデザインを追求するために、その場で行われる活動を深く尊重することである。

ボーズリーの主な魅力の一つは、そのために彼はニューヨークを舞台にした小説のヒーローにでもなれそうなのだが、自分の間違いを素直に認めることであり、その間違いとは特に彼がランドスケープ・アーキテクチャーのコミュニティーから距離をおいてきたことであり、彼等から賛同を得ることに興味を持ってこなかったことである。今やチームスポーツを尊重できるようになったボーズリーは公共事業でのチームワークについて知るようになってきたが、その一方彼の個人主義的な側面は、彼のオフィスでの仕事のパートナーシップを分解することになる、アーバン・ランドスケープへの燃え上がるようなしかし彼のものとは上手く噛み合わない情熱に、気づきはじめたのだった。彼はまた一人に戻ったが、今回はもっと深い意味でそうなのだった。「私は群衆心理のわなにはまることを恐れていたのだと思う。そしてただひたすら身を潜めてデザインと実験の旅に向かった。ヨーロッパのアーバンプラザの方式もそのアメリカ版も、それらを勉強はしたものの、賛同する気にはなれなかった。それらは多様な文化背景を持つアーバンスペースには殆んど適さないと信じていたからである。決して、私は「ランドスケープアーキテクチャー」誌に自分のプロジェクトを提出したりASLA賞に応募したりしなかった。今になってみるとそれは近視眼的だった!」このように影響を受けることを拒む態度は、多分まだ自分自身のデザイン理論を形成したり自分の声を見つけたりしようとしている者に特有なのであろう。

こうした彼の思考の枠組みについてもう少し付記しておくことは大切であろう。なぜならこの近視眼のおかげでボーズリーは彼のより広い視野を保持したからである。その自己防衛的性格のおかげで、彼の考え方はは常に柔軟であり、いかなるスタイルやドグマにもはまらず、適用性に応じて古典からモダンそしてオーガニックに至るまでそれら全てを活用できるという絶対的自信を持ち得たと言える。彼の大学卒業後の成長は直観と発見を通じてなされ、その自己防御性の故に彼の価値基準は常に明白であった。「第一に、私は都市生活のクオリティーを改善したかった。それが今でも私が最も気をくばることである。」そして彼はいつも自分に正直であった。「たといいくら同僚から受け入れられて、どんなに個展を開いたり賞をもらったとしても、全ての階層の人々で埋まった、私がデザインしたスペースを逍遙することで得られる誇りと満足に優るものはない」とボーズリーは現在も信じている。「私はいまだに、たとえそれではデザイン賞を取れないものであっても、人々の楽しみと親近感の度合いが高ければ、その公共オープンスペースを評価する。」今日では、ボーズリーは彼が影響をうけた人々の名前を喜んで列挙する。デザインのプロセスのレヴェルではウィリアム・ホワイト、ジョン・オルムスビー・サイモンド、ヒデオ・ササキ、そしてカール・リン、デザインではポール・フリードバーグ、ダン・カイリー、ローレンス・ハルプリン、イサム・ノグチ、ピーター・ウォーカー、そして1980年代のスペインのカタローニャ地方のデザイナーたちがそこに含まれている。

ついにボーズリーの時がやって来た。「私はそれがいつだったかは分からないが、ある時ニューヨークの開発業者が私を見いだした。」そして彼等はボーズリーに接近していった。彼が彼等の言うことに耳を傾けたからである。「デザインの仕事を請け負うために彼等に媚び諂うことはしなかった。」ボーズリーは彼等とコミュニティーの食い違った目標を理解し、いかに双方を満足させるデザインが可能かを呈示した。ニューヨークのように反対運動の活発な地域でそれを行うことはやさしいことではない。

イーストリバー遊歩道公園のような近隣地区改善は、開発業者が公共オープンスペースに手を伸ばすときの敷地として良い例である。この公園は、環境へのインパクト査定の結果要求された環境緩和策であり、また、1960年代に遡るもののニューヨーク市が新しい公共オープンスペースを産み出すために開発業者たちにさらなる容積率を約束した1980年代に盛んに行われた、いわゆ

る「ボーナスプラザ」でもある。より広い床面積(普通は建物の高さを増すことで解決される)を得る代りに、開発業者たちは、市の都市計画課によって定められたガイドラインに沿うように作られた全くパブリックなアーバンプラザを提供し、それを維持管理するのである。ボーズリーによれば、初期に設定されたガイドラインは数々の不毛のプラザを産み出すのみで、その利点と言えば将来デザインし直されるための土地を確保したにすぎない。しかし、時を経るにしたがってそのガイドラインは人々のアメニティーとアクセスの必用条件を加えて洗練され、強力なものとなった。

新しくて便利なオープンスペース建設の可能性をほとんど見いだせない都市で仕事をしていながら、ボーズリーはそうしたスペースの重要性とデザインのチャンスを予想した数少ないランドスケープ・アーキテクトたちの一人である。増加した容積率(FARs)のおかげで大きな利潤が得られるので、開発業者たちは大抵オープンスペースにかかるコストを気にしない。もし彼等がそれを安くあげようとしたらどうであろうか?「もしパブリックスペースの質の点で妥協に他ならないと私が感じることを彼等がしようとしたら、私はいつもニューヨーク市の都市計画ガイドラインを指し示すことができる。成功した公園やプラザは市にとって利益となり、もしそれらがきちんと維持されれば彼等の物件にも付加価値を与えるのだと、ほとんどの開発業者たちは理解している。そのために私は天国にでもいるような心地でいられる。気前の良い施主のために働きながら公共のために尽くすことが出来るからである。それは双方にとって成功する状況なのである。」

その開発業者との出会いの後たった一年のうちにボーズリーは13のボーナスプラザを手がけ、現在までにマンハッタン内に30以上完成させた。今日彼はそのうちのいくつかを自己批判する。それらがあまりにコンテクスチャルだからである。「私のコンテクストの定義は狭義的字義的すぎた。」たとえそれらのプラザに際立った性格が欠けていても、パブリックスペースとしての成功に彼は満足し、もし真剣な批判を加えるとしても、時折それらが建物に従属しすぎていてプライヴェートな場所に見えてしまうことぐらいであろう。しかしながら、マンハッタプレイス、100UNプラザ、そしてシェラソン・リーマン・ガーデンは大成功したオープンスペースである。それらは都市の聖域であり、現在の知的認識から生まれた庭であり、実際には文化を表明する環境の中に自然というコンセプチュアルな概念を埋め込んでいる。つまり、それらは,植物,水、そして石を複雑な形のデザインに用いて、都市の錯綜から静かに避難する場所を創り出している。ジェネラルモータース・ビルディング・プラザやパラマウント・プラザ、そして、ニューヨーク市内の公共オープンスペースへの彼のデザイン上の貢献を認めてボーズリー・パークと改名されたシェフィールド・プラザなどといった、1960年代に建設されて立派ではあるが不毛のプラザの多くをデザインするために、今日ボーズリーが起用されていることは良い知らせである。こうしてデザインし直された数々のプラザは、空間創出へのボーズリーの新しいアプローチを反映し、上手く行けば他のデザイナーたちが彼の後を追うようになるぐらい刺激を提供するであろう。

ボーズリーは彼のデザインの閃きを1985年に行ったスペインのバルセロナへの旅に帰する。そこで彼は1992年のオリンピックに向けて準備されていた都市改造に啓発された。ニューヨークでの楽ではない経験があるが故に、「伝統に深く根付いたある都市に21世紀に向けてのデザイン的跳躍を仕向けることが出来る」という事実に感嘆した。バルセロナの開化されたパスクアル・マラガル市長と彼の相談役である建築家オリエル・ボヒラスは「同市のための大きな一連の街並み、公園、そしてプラザの改善案を創出し、それらの全ては私がニューヨークで夢見て実現させようとしていたものだった」とボーズリーは語る。そこで実現されたランドスケープに彼が見たものは「人に刺激を与え精神を鼓舞する人間精神の表現であり、カタローニャ地方のアートとデザインに特徴的な即興性と混ざった、モダニズム的秩序と構成の空間であった。」前衛デザインを妨げるのではなく、市の役人たちはそれを要求し、全ての官僚政治的な障害を取り除いた。

ボーズリーはそこでデザインを文化的に支えるものに最も印象を受けた。「人生に関してのカタローニャ地方の哲学は一般常識や物事をやり遂げることを意味するセーナ(sena)と騒々しい馬鹿馬鹿しさや芸術的創造を意味するラウクサ(rauxa)が混ざったものである。」ボーズリーにとってバ

ルセロナ訪問は、彼の性格やデザインのアプローチのやり方における対立項を理解するために自分自身が変容していくような経験であり、それはカタローニャ文化全体のデザイン哲学に反映されているようである。「私はカタローニャ人として生まれたような気がした。」バルセロナから発信されているデザインのアイデアは、自己中心的な芸術表現ではなく、そこには公共デザインへの思い入れがあった。ランドスケープ・アーキテクトたちは芸術と社会意識、そしてデザインと政治的意識を統合することが出来るのだということを、バルセロナは証明している。

1980年代のボーズリーのより大胆なデザインアプローチは、その時期に初めて経済的安定を彼が感じたという事実に依るところもある。ニューヨークに移住して以来、彼の懸念は最初は経済的サバイバルであり、後には拠点の構築であった。しかしながら、そうこうしているうちに1987年の株価暴落が起こった。そしてそれはあたかも彼の言葉を借りれば「私の足下からカーペットを引っこ抜く」かのようであった。ボーズリーは経済的危機から精神的疲労を伴って脱出したが、その時、ある今までとは異なる展望を持っていた。「私は決して金持ちにはならないだろう。それなら、私の貧困に対する恐れに付随した全ての否定的エネルギーを、自分の芸術的使命と私が過去十五年間構築してきた確固たるデザイン理論に向けようではないか。」

ボーズリーのデザインの変容はまた、彼が一連の巨大で重要なコミッションを受け取ったときにも起こった。このうちのいくつかの現場は日本で、そこには大阪の世界貿易センターやボーズリーによる四つの多彩な彫刻を取り入れた東京のゲートシティーが含まれる。しかし、そのほとんどはニューヨークにおいてであり、特に、崩壊しつつあるウォーターフロントに代表される放置されたスペースを見直そうという、アメリカの多くの他の都市と共通する社会的運動から生まれたプロジェクトであった。この動きの中で、ボーズリーはいくつもの、ニューヨークで最もすばらしい公園をデザインした。彼のより大胆なデザインをするという決定にはすばらしい結果が伴い、そのデザイン上の変遷は、1984年に始まって11年間続き、そのデザインの手がかりがバッテリーパークシティーから取られたイーストリバー遊歩道公園のような初期の作品から、現在進行中のチェルシー・ウォーターサイド・パーク、ガントリー・プラザ・ステート・パーク、そしてロックフェラー大学のサウスキャンパスに至るまでのスタイルの変化に見て取れる。

ガントリープラザでは、四つの飛び出した埠頭、敷地の工業的残骸、そして陸地(研磨されて形があり構築された)から水(より荒れていながら、それでいていっそうはかない)への移行、これらの全てが今ではコンテクストとは関係を持たないある哲学を表明している。ある批評でニューヨークタイムスの建築批評家ハーバート・ミュシャンは、なぜガントリー・プラザが特別な場所かをレトリカルに問う。彼によれば「なぜならそれが未知の世界を明らかにするからであり、ガストン・バシェラールが<空間の詩>と呼んだ、イメージや関係性、発見、そして驚きによって構成された内面的世界へ、ボーズリー氏が踏み込んでいっているからである。巣。貝殻。ミニチュア。暗示された茫漠。外側と内側の弁証法。これらはみなバシェラールが唱えたコンセプトである。それらがここでは、多様で豊富な形態によって空間化されているのが分かる。」

ボーズリーの過去十年の仕事は、コンテクスチャリズムも伝統主義もひたすら盲目的に規定されてきたという批判的確信から出発している。「ニューヨークは芸術と創造性の世界的中心であるという名声があるにもかかわらず、同市内の公共の建築物とランドスケープは、新鮮なアイデアや前衛的ヴィジョンをゆっくりと粉にして平凡なスープにしてしまう公共公開討議の善意的なプロセスの、痛ましくも保守的な産物である。コンセンサスを求めて、また、上手く行く他のプロトタイプを見つけられずに、行政の担当者たちは、往々にしてセントラルパークのような19世紀のランドスケープをメランコリックに参照するという、最も人々の反対を受けない道程に引き戻してしまう。キャリアがかかっていない他所からのデザイナーたちを除いて、この様な状況は他と違っていようとするデザイナーたちに報酬を与える環境ではない。反対に、彼等は通常、投石器と弓矢の標的にされてデザインのシベリアに送られてしまう。」こうした態度は、ボーズリーが最も大切なゴー

ルだと強く感じているもの、つまり、空間の持つ意味、「その意味の我々の現在の文化や未来の世代との関係性、そしてその意味が人間精神に触れて我々の先入観や限りのある想像力の境界を越えて我々を鼓舞すること、にとって有害である。」「我々は責任に加えて、都市環境を築いていくにあたって単に適切である以上の大きな役割を果たすための可能性を持っている。」

「思考のない、感覚の鈍い形態操作」にはボーズリーは強く反対する。「私の仕事はいまだに適切性を主張する内なるヒューマニスティックな声によって導かれている。それは人々に仕え、意味を持たなければならない。公共オープンスペースは神聖な土地であり、我々は無理やり公共委託委員会を尊重するように仕向けられていると、私は考える。公共オープンスペースは、デモクラシーの理想から発っする行為のための貴重な場であり、実にいかなる社会的、文化的そして経済的境界もないメルティングポットであり、それゆえデザインにとって究極のチャレンジなのである。」都市生活の現実にさらされているオープンスペースのいかなる長期的成功も、幅広い層の人々が利用できることにかかっている。「公聴会で<公園の望ましくない使われ方>についてコメントする少数の人々の言うことだけでなく、犬の散歩をする人やローラーブレーダーのような、そのスペースが彼等の日々の生活に密着しているあらゆる人々の意見に」デザイナーたちは耳を傾けなければならない。

こうしたプログラムや社会的確信と混ざりあって、ボーズリーは「他にも同様に尊重すべき事柄があり、それによって我々はショックを得たり、驚いたり、我々自身を目覚ましたり、意識を呼び覚ましたり、精神を昂揚させたりしなければならない。」因習を打破するような解釈か、または隠喩的な解釈を利用することで、彼の作品は、単に自然だけではなく我々の時代の文化のイメージを強く反映している。「私はいつもヴァナキュウラーなアーバン・ランドスケープを洗練させられる新しい形態を追求している。もし我々の仕事が他の時代の偉大な仕事と比較されるとしたら、それは何かを言えなければならないし、<いつこの場所は作られたのか?>という問いに対して答えられなければならない。」ボーズリーはこれを成し遂げるための様々なアイデアを持っている。例えば、それはヴィデオ通信における技術発達を利用することである。「テレビとインターネットが、人々が公共の場で集まる機会を減少させてきたのに対して、屋外ヴィデオスクリーンは、ホーリー・ホワイトの小説に出てくる曲芸士が三角模様によって見知らぬ人々を結び付けてしまうように、人々を引き付けることによって、打ち捨てられたアーバンスペースに活気を呼び戻す文化的アイコンになれる。」時には、都会の敷地を対象に仕事をするデザイナーの最も大きなチャレンジは、控え目であること、つまり自分がデザインしたいという欲求を抑制して都会のエネルギーが自身を表現するのに任せることであることを、ボーズリーは我々に気付かせる。「私はいつも都会のすばらしい活動のためのステージセットを作ろうとしている。そのスペースでは、人々は多くの感情を経験し、様々な生を生き、即興で何かをしたり、日々の雑事から解放されるのである。」

このステージのイメージは、ボーズリーのデザイン哲学の中心にあるようだ。それはいくつかの理由によるが、第一に挙げられるのはプロジェクトのプロセスの問題である。ボーズリーは、あるプロジェクトに対して一般の人々からの賛同を得るそのプロセスの重要性を強調する。この都会での活動の一幕は非常に重みがある。「デザインのコンセプトはいくつかのダイアグラムから来るのではない。それは複雑なダイアグラムの中で混ざり合い、発酵するのである。こうした公共の賛同を得るプロセスの中でデザインコンセプトを形成するにあたっては、意見の拡張と対立、流動化、そして中核となるアイデアを吸収したり変換したりしながらもそれを守る根本的態度を包含する、心の余裕がなければならない。この流動性の故にこうした態度は、決断力がなくデザイン原理を放棄しているように見えるかも知れないが、公聴会の束縛の中でデザインコンセプトを守り抜くためには実際のところ必要不可欠なのである。」ボーズリーはこのプロセスを、デザイナー、施主、そして住民の間の協力であり、それによってあるデザインのアイデアが単なるアーティストの意向から現実化に向けてはぐくまれるのだと考える。理想的状況下ではランドスケープ・アーキテクトというのは、役者のパフォーマンスに承諾を与えると同時に彼の意図の中核は保持する舞台監督のようである。幸いにも、プロセスを大切にすることを重んじながら直観に恵まれたデザイナーとして、プロジェクトのプログラムと敷地の条件を融合させることによって、ボーズリーは一つの創造的アプローチを発展させてきた。その融合とは、コンセプトや形態表現に先んずる発酵であり、それは事務所の中でや、他のプロフェッショナルな人々やアーティストと一緒に、また公共の委員会と共同で仕事をするときに威力を発揮する。

ステージのイメージがボーズリーのデザインの根幹にあると言える第二の理由は、彼の新旧の仕事を見れば明らかである。彼の作品の審美的力強さにもかかわらず、その構成要素の一つ一つが浮き上がってしまうことはない。大阪のゲートシティーにある新しい彫刻であろうと、波のベンチ、フィッシング・テーブル、座席の高く据えられた椅子、そして長椅子といった、ガントリー・プラザ・ステート・パークの埠頭に設置された数々の滑稽なフォリーであろうと、それぞれのエレメントが見る者をその空間へと魅了する。この公園では、手すりや腰掛け、彫刻、そしてフォリーは単に空間を規定するだけではなく、受動的な観察者を能動的な役者に変えてしまうのである。ボーズリーの仕事には秩序ある枠組みとしてのフォーマリズムを見ることが出来るが、そこでは、時には調和とバランスと共に、しかしより頻繁には、個体性とオーガニックな流動性、人工と自然、パターンとそこからの驚きを伴う逸脱、そして<セーナ>と<ラウクサ>といった対現象の間で双方が溶融する場所を探求するかのように、形象と物体性とが重なりあっている。そして、アーバン・ランドスケープにおける芸術と意味との包括であるところの、社会目的と施主の目標、そして芸術的表現の三つの統合をそこに見ることが出来る一方で、ボーズリーのアートの根底に横たわるテーマは、人間の行動に変容を与えることである。「アーバンスペースでの我々の仕事は、数百万人もの生活に多大な影響を及ぼすことができるのだということに、ほとんどのランドスケープ・アーキテクトたちは気付いていない。」

この言葉を心に留めると、我々は違った目でニューヨークを見れるだろう。上空からマンハッタンを見下ろすと、壊れやすそうな建築群の真ん中にセントラルパークの緑色の形が見える。それはニューヨークのアーバンスペースにおいて否定しがたい事実としてあり、19世紀の偉大な歴史的文化遺物である。地上に立つと、その強固さと威圧性によって圧倒されてしまいそうな数々の構築物に囲まれて、時々、全く緑地を見ないこともある。しかし、もし緑地を見ることがあっても、それらはあまりに往々にしてフレデリック・ロウ・オルムステッドの長く続く、しかし非常に薄まった影響を見せている。マンハッタンにおける緑地の不足とそこで見られる過去の死んだ手法との両方を、数百もの都会の場所が現代のランドスケープ・アーキテクトたちのアートを待ち構えているのだという事実の証拠として、我々は多分楽観的に受けとめなければならない。そしてそれらの場所とは、ボーズリーが呼ぶところの「活気に満ちた都会の共同体の社会的混ぜ鉢」になりうるのである。こうした将来性のある場所の計画は現実化するだろうか?それらはどの様な様相を呈するのだろうか? そのデザイナーたちは伝統に依拠した平凡さという安全な道に固執するだろうか?または、この都市を21世紀にふさわしいものにし続けるような公園やプラザ、そして街並みを彼等は創造するだろうか?

この点の将来については我々は楽観的でいられる。なぜなら、トーマス・ボーズリーは1969年以来ニューヨーク市の地図上に彼の足跡を残し、しかも彼のキャリアはいまだ始まったばかりだからである。彼がデザインした一番最近のアーバンステージは、今まさに我々が座っている場所のそばにあるかもしれない。そして我々はそれが、すり減った過去に向かってではなく、わくわくするような未来に向かって訴えかけるものであろうと確信できる。ボーズリーは彼のユニークなデザインの過程を見い出したが、彼が最も優れたランドスケープ・アーキテクトたちを代表しているがゆえに、我々は、将来他のランドスケープ・アーキテクトたちも彼を見習って勇気ある一歩を踏み出し、アートの方向へ進むであろうという期待を持つことが出来るのである。

翻訳: 金 一 (コロンビア大学大学院、博士過程、西洋建築史専攻)
Translation: Il Kim, Ph.D. candidate, Columbia University.

Photographers
Thomas Balsley
12abcdefghijkl, 13mno, 23fj, 32, 33ab, 35,
37b, 39a, 42, 44, 45b, 72acdefhjkl,
73abcdfgkl, 74afhjl, 75cg, 84

Louis Checkman
73h

Scott Frances/ESTO
74n

Samuel Lawrence
59

Kokyu Miwa
36, 37a, 40, 41, 43

Michael Moran
28, 29, 30, 31, 74d

Bo Parker
72m

Jock Pottle
58, 60, 61, 75a

Cervin Robinson
45a, 46abc, 47abc, 48-49

Betsy Pinover Schiff
Front cover, 18, 21, 23abcdeghik, 24, 25, 26,
27abcd, 34, 73e, 74bi

Steven Tupu
63a

William Webb
50, 53, 54, 74k

Renderers
Keith Crawford
62, 63b, 75klm

Edwin Evalle
75j

Octavio Figueroa
72bg

Richard Hoyen
56, 66, 74cem, 75def

Kevin Woest
73j, 74g

Modelmakers
Wally Sokolowski
58, 60, 61, 73hm, 75a

Graphic Design
Red Square Design